Introduction to Accounting

Harold Edey LLD (Hon.), BCom., FCA is Professor of Accounting at the London School of Economics in the University of London. Before becoming a university teacher he was an assistant investment manager in a large financial group. He is a chartered accountant and is a member of the Council of the Institute of Chartered Accountants in England and Wales, of the Institute's Students Education and Training Committee, of the Accounting Standards Committee and of the Inflation Accounting Steering Group. He has been a member of the Council of National Academic Awards and was chairman of its Arts and Social Studies Committee. He is the author of *Business Budgets and Accounts*, co-author of *National Income and Social Accounting*, and co-editor of other works.

By the same author

National Income and Social Accounting
(with Professor Alan T. Peacock and Ronald Cooper)
Business Budgets and Accounts

Introduction to Accounting

Harold C. Edey

Professor of Accounting at the London
School of Economics and Political Science
in the University of London

Hutchinson of London

Hutchinson & Co (Publishers) Ltd
3 Fitzroy Square, London W1P 6JD

London Melbourne Sydney Auckland
Wellington Johannesburg and agencies
throughout the world

First published 1963
Second edition 1964
Reprinted 1966, 1967 and 1969
Third edition 1973
Reprinted 1975
Fourth edition 1978
Reprinted 1979

Set in Monotype Times New Roman
Printed in Great Britain at The Anchor Press Ltd
and bound by Wm Brendon & Son Ltd,
both of Tiptree, Essex

ISBN 0 09 132580 3 (cased)
     0 09 132581 1 (paper)

Contents

Preface to fourth edition

As I indicated in the preface to the first edition of this book, I have aimed at providing the beginner with a grounding in the basic ideas and methods of accounting without cluttering up his mind with unnecessary detail or unnecessarily lengthy examples.

If I have been successful, the relatively simple examples used, combined with the discussion, will provide him or her with patterns of thought that can readily be transferred to the complexity of financial work in real life, or to more advanced work, or both.

The level of approach is suitable for students beginning education for professional accounting, for graduates and undergraduates beginning specialist and non-specialist courses in universities and polytechnics, and for persons reading on their own who need an introduction to the elements of the subject. It represents about one term's work.

I have taken the opportunity offered by the need for a substantial revision to include a new chapter on current cost accounting, a topic which no one who intends to become an accountant, or to be concerned with accounting data, can now afford to neglect.

It has seemed to me for some time that it might be useful to consolidate the introductory material on double entry into a chapter on its own and this I have now done.

I have also added a short introductory chapter and have extended considerably the chapter on fixed assets.

1 Introduction

Accounting exists because at any one time the resources available to satisfy the needs of human beings are limited. These resources have to be *allocated* or *managed* in order to secure their best use and avoid their waste. Accounting is an aid in this management and in the sharing of the products. It is a set of concepts and methods for making and recording measurements relating to these matters, classifying and summarizing them, and finally reporting and interpreting the results.

The main functions of accounting can be grouped as follows:

The 'memory function'

Any organization, and most persons, need in varying degrees to keep records of the money they have from time to time, of the debts owed to or by them, and of the various physical objects and legal rights they possess or are entitled to. In a business organization, or a public authority, or a charity of any size, this need is insistent and calls for the keeping of accurate, accessible and up-to-date records. We call these records the 'books of account', though nowadays the 'books' may be punched cards or magnetic tapes or microfilm fiches, and so on.

These records constitute the financial memory of the organization. Not only must they be kept, they must also be designed to avoid fraud and error, so far as this is possible.

The design and maintenance of such records is, and always has been, a major function of accountancy from the most ancient times. Archaeological finds suggest that the art of writing itself developed in the ancient world from the need for them. In modern accountancy this kind of work tends to be described as the analysis and design of *accounting systems*.

Measurement for 'sharing'

A second major function of accounting arises out of the fact that usually more than one person has an interest in the results of economic activities. Companies have shareholders. Partnerships have partners. The tax authorities have an interest in the profits of all businesses. The state has an interest in the results of state industries. Management remuneration and workers' bonuses may depend upon financial results. Employees have a general interest in those results. And so on. There is therefore a need for an acceptable procedure for determining an agreed amount as the 'surplus available for sharing out' in a given year. This procedure must be reasonably objective. There must be a limit to the discretion left to those who determine the results.

Generally accepted or 'standard' accounting rules or practices have arisen for this reason. They have been created partly by practice and custom and partly by legal rules (which themselves have usually arisen from past practice and views arising out of that practice). Carefully thought out general theory has not played a great part in their development. Furthermore, rules vary according to the use to be made of the figures they produce. For example, 'profit' for tax purposes does not in general equal 'profit' reported to shareholders, because there are special legal rules governing tax assessments. Thus, in a specified set of circumstances there may be more than one possible 'correct' figure of profit, dependent on the purpose for which it is required. However, it is to profit reported to shareholders that standard practices are primarily directed, and it is this profit figure which is generally regarded as 'the profit' of a company.

Such profit figures must be regarded as convenient but conventional assessments. For this reason they have disadvantages when used for other purposes than those for which they were developed. For instance, they do not provide an 'absolute' or 'correct' assessment of the financial results of a business such that they can be used uncritically for financial planning of future operations, or for judging the results of these. Nevertheless, because they are often the only figures available, they are used continually for these purposes. Their limitations are not always appreciated and there is plenty of scope for improvement, even for their primary purpose of sharing. It is therefore desirable for anyone concerned with financial matters to learn how they are prepared and how they can be used.

Management planning and control

A third major function of accounting is the provision of a schematic financial 'model' of an organization, linking together, and providing the framework for understanding, the financial aspects of what is often a complex set of activities. This function is of great assistance in the process of planning and control, and helps to reduce the risk of internal inconsistency of action in different parts of the organization where there is delegation of authority.

Linked to this process of *budgetary planning and control* of the business as a whole is the analysis of the financial effects of sectional activities inside the business. This provides detailed controls to reduce waste of resources and helps to improve decisions through better understanding of the relation between particular actions and the absorption of resources they cause.

The future

As time passes the accounting methods used in the above functions, and particularly those concerned with function (3), will without doubt be more closely integrated than at present is usual with scientifically devised planning models, based on financial decision theory, which are now being increasingly used in business. If this is correct, accounting will more and more appear in the guise of statistical reporting, cast in the same form as the models. This development still lies some way ahead. It seems likely to take the form of restructuring accounting rather than a root and branch change, for much of the accounting information now collected and reported upon will continue to be essential. Proposals for the introduction of current value or current cost accounting, discussed in Chapter 12, are a move in this direction.

Aims of this book

The first step in the study of all these matters is to get a good understanding of (*a*) the statements that can be said to form the basis of all accounting, the balance sheet and the profit and loss account; and of (*b*) the rules of double entry accounting, which all accountants know and use. This is what this book is about.

The accounting needs of different organizations vary according to their functions and the way in which they obtain their finance. It is, however, easy to exaggerate the differences and there are basic principles that apply to all situations. The accounting problems of any person or organization can be tackled successfully if the principles are well understood. As it is not possible in one book to study the problems of all kinds of organization, a selection has to be made. Here the examples refer mainly to business activities in the private sector. The examples given are simplified and many of the results obtained in them could have been reached by what may seem to be more direct methods. The purpose of the examples, however, is to illustrate methods that are useful, or indeed essential, in the more complex cases that arise in practice. Simple examples are used in order to avoid lengthy arithmetic and copying that would not contribute to the understanding of principles.

In order to save space the figures in the examples represent lower money values than would be found in real life. Readers who wish to make the various quantities more 'realistic' can imagine the application of appropriate multiplying factors.

The economic and accounting problems of any organization are strongly influenced by the legal framework within which it operates. They are similarly influenced by the general financial background. Readers may find that the study of one of two of the introductory texts on these matters given in the reading list at the end a useful complement to the study of the book. The reading list also suggests more advanced texts for those who wish to carry the study further.

2 Balance sheets

The *balance sheet* is the fundamental statement of accounting. All other accounting statements can be regarded as derived either from a balance sheet or from a comparison of two balance sheets, real or imaginary, at different points of time.

A balance sheet is an ordered statement of:

1 a set of economic resources or *assets*, each with a value set upon it; and
2 the financial *claims* of persons or organizations on the amount of value represented by those assets.

Since all assets are, by definition, owned by someone, the total claims just exhaust the value of the assets. Another way of describing the claims is to say that they represent the way in which the holding of the assets is *financed*.

Let us consider an individual, *A*. Let us suppose that his private balance sheet at a given moment of time is as follows:

Assets

	£
House	10,000
Investments	500
Cash (money)*	50
	10,550

Claims or finance

	£
Creditors	1,500
Ownership interest	9,050
	10,550

* Accountants usually call all money 'cash', whether in the form of coin, notes, bank balances, or cheques not yet paid into the bank. Exceptions are coin and notes held for minor payments, which are called 'petty cash'.

This balance sheet shows:

1 The assets owned by A, and the money values set on these: in total £10,550.
2 The amount owing by A to creditors: in other words the claims of third parties against A: £1,500. These claims are called A's *liabilities*.
3 A's residual claim on the assets, the difference between 1 and 2: £9,050. We shall call this A's *ownership interest*. Other terms that can be used are *wealth* or *capital*.

Usually one would expect A's assets to be greater than the claims against them (apart from his own residual ownership interest). If the reverse were true, A's wealth would be negative; he would then, at the time of the balance sheet, owe more than he could pay, always assuming that the assets were shown at the value which they would fetch if they were sold. In these circumstances he would be *insolvent* and might be made bankrupt if he were suddenly called upon to pay his debts.

An important thing to notice about the balance sheet is that it balances; that is to say, the total value of the assets is equal to the total value of the claims or finance. This is because the ownership interest always makes up the difference between the asset values and the liabilities to outsiders. The amount of the owner's interest shown in the balance sheet depends upon the assessment made by A, or by his accountant, of the value of the assets and of the amount of the liabilities. In practice this assessment often raises problems. However, for the time being we shall avoid these in order to concentrate upon the nature of the balance sheet and of the other statements that can be derived from it. We shall assume that the assets in the balance sheet, other than cash, are taken at their saleable value, and that the liabilities are stated at the amount needed to pay them off.

Finance

The balance sheet demonstrates that, for every economic resource that A possesses, someone must provide finance: in other words, the total value of the assets held by A represents the provision of finance of exactly equal amount, either by A himself, or by outsiders, or by both. A can only hold assets amounting to £10,550 if he himself, or creditors to whom he owes money, or both, are prepared to forgo spending money on other things. This apparently trivial statement is of great economic importance. It draws attention, first to the deliberate choice made by A to have the particular collection of assets shown in his balance sheet rather than to spend the money he could get by selling these on personal consumption or on a different collection of assets; and secondly to an important limiting factor in all economic affairs, namely that control of additional economic resources can only be obtained if someone is prepared (or is forced) to sacrifice for the time being the disposition of purchasing power that he could otherwise have enjoyed.

Let us now suppose that A wants to buy a boat costing £500. His balance sheet shows that, except for the £50, he has no ready money. If he does not want to spend his cash or sell some of his investments, he can have the boat only if extra finance is provided by someone else.

This can be expressed schematically by showing his balance sheet as it would appear if he bought the boat. The boat and the new finance are shown in italics. We have:

Assets

	£
House	10,000
Investments	500
Cash	50
Boat	*500*
	11,050

Finance

	£
Creditors	1,500
Ownership interest	9,050
New finance needed	*500*
	11,050

By putting the boat among the assets we have created a gap in the claims section of the balance sheet which must be filled by new finance. If someone gives A a present of £500, this new finance will become part of A's ownership interest: he can then finance the boat himself. If he borrows the money, the new finance represents an additional liability of A to a finance company or a bank or someone else. Whoever provides the money will have to forgo other possible expenditure (unless the money is borrowed, in turn, from yet a third person, and so on).

Transaction analysis

Let us now return to A's original balance sheet (i.e. before the boat was bought) and examine the effect of some transactions over a period of time. Let us assume the balance sheet was drawn up on Wednesday night. On Thursday A spends £20 on food and entertainment. His cash will therefore fall by £20. He has gained no other asset.*

The new balance sheet, on Thursday night, will be:

	£
House	10,000
Investments	500
Cash	30
	10,530

	£
Creditors	1,500
Ownership	9,030
	10,530

The effect of this change is to reduce the total claim by A himself against the assets, that is, his ownership interest, by £20. This now appears as £9,030 instead of £9,050.

On Friday, let us say, A receives £150 in respect of his salary for the week, and he repays £100 of the £1,500 he owes. The net effect of these two transactions on his cash will be to increase it by £50. He now owes £100 less to his creditors, however. Hence his ownership interest has risen by more than the amount of the net increase in cash. It has in fact risen by £150.

On Saturday, A spends £10 on food and entertainment and £40 on improving the house. As £40 out of the £50 spent may be assumed to increase the value of the house, A's ownership interest only falls by £10, the amount spent on the benefits that are assumed to have disappeared as soon as they have been enjoyed. The net decrease in his cash it is true is £50; but the asset 'house' rises by £40; and his ownership interest falls only by the difference, £10.

* In a sense, of course, A has acquired an asset, since his personal pleasure is increased; but this asset is presumably of short durability. For practical purposes it is ignored.

His balance sheets on the four consecutive days will read as follows:

	Wed £	Thurs £	Fri £	Sat £
House	10,000	10,000	10,000	10,040
Investments	500	500	500	500
Cash	50	30	80	30
	10,550	10,530	10,580	10,570
Creditors	1,500	1,500	1,400	1,400
Ownership interest	9,050	9,030	9,180	9,170
	10,550	10,530	10,580	10,570

Here we have a set of statements summarizing what has happened to *A*'s finances during this period. These tell the tale much more quickly and concisely than is possible in words.

Funds statements

A slightly different picture can be given if, instead of the actual balance sheets, we show the differences in each class of asset and in each source of finance, between succeeding balance sheets:

	Wed– Thurs £	Thurs– Fri £	Fri– Sat £	Wed– Sat £
House	–	–	+40	+40
Investments	–	–	–	–
Cash	–20	+50	–50	–20
	–20	+50	–10	+20
Creditors	–	–100	–	–100
Ownership interest	–20	+150	–10	+120
	–20	+50	–10	+20

Statements of this kind, showing period-to-period changes in assets and finance, are called *statements of sources and uses of funds* or, more shortly, *funds statements*. They provide summaries of the way in which finance has been made available and how it has been used during a period.

If the funds statement for the period from Wednesday to Saturday were presented by an accountant as a *report* to *A* (or to some other person, such as *A*'s banker) it would usually be set out on the following lines, so as to emphasize the net sources of increased finance during the period and the net uses of that increase:

Funds statement, Wednesday to Saturday

Sources of funds	£
Income *less* expenditure on consumption	120
Reduction in cash available	20
	140

Uses of funds	
Improvement of house	40
Repayment of creditors	100
	140

An alternative presentation would allow the change in cash to emerge as a net difference between the other sources and uses, thus:

Sources of funds	£
Income *less* expenditure on consumption	120

Uses of funds	
Improvement of house	40
Repayment of creditors	100
	140

Reduction in cash available	20

The receipts and payments of cash – the *cash flows* – have special significance because cash is an asset that can be used immediately for any purpose, whereas before the finance locked up in other assets can be released they must be sold. This takes time. Furthermore, the cash released by the sale tends to be less, the shorter the time allowed for the transaction – i.e. the sooner the cash is needed.

Cash flows are so important that a good business management will nearly always require statements summarizing these to be prepared at short intervals. In outline such a statement would look something like the following, though in practice the receipts and payments would probably each be split up to show their main elements:

	Wed–Thurs £	Thurs–Fri £	Fri–Sat £	Wed–Sat £
Receipts	–	150	–	150
Payments	20	100	50	170
Change in balance*	−20	+50	−50	−20
Balance at end	30	80	30	30

Income and expenditure

Another set of figures of particular significance can be extracted from the funds statement: the net difference in each period between *income* and *expenditure on consumption*. In this particular case the income is the gain in resources that *A* receives as the result of his daily occupation: his salary. The expenditure on consumption is the amount he has spent on the purchase of such things as food, clothing, entertainment (but *not* on improving his house. The amount spent on this has increased its value and is called *investment*). The difference between income and consumption is *saving*, and reflects the increase in *A*'s capital or wealth. On days when consumption exceeds income saving will be negative.

Because of the special significance of income and expenditure, *A* may wish to have an *income and expenditure statement* prepared. This would be drawn up on the following lines:

	Wed–Thurs £	Thurs–Fri £	Fri–Sat £	Wed–Sat £
Income	–	150	–	150
Consumption	20	–	10	30
Saving	−20	+150	−10	+120

Here again, in practice the rows could be sub-divided to show the various components of income and saving. Note that the saving in each period is *not* the same as the cash change in the same period. The income and expenditure statement tells a different story from the cash statement.

---

* The amount of an asset held (or of a liability owed) at a given point of time is called a *balance*.

The financial statements we have discussed in this chapter relate to magnitudes – income, consumption, saving, investment – that we should find in national income statistics. They are, however, similar in pattern to the statements that, in one form or another, are used throughout business, in public departments, and generally in all organizations involved in economic activity. Some of the terms used in these contexts differ a little from those in this chapter, as we shall see when we come to business accounts. The basic ideas remain the same whatever the activities depicted. A summary of changes in assets and claims in successive *balance sheets* forms a *funds statement*; changes in cash through time can be set out in greater or less detail in a *cash statement*; growth or decay in the ownership interest can be shown in an *income and expenditure* statement (which in a business is usually called a *profit and loss statement*, or just an *income statement*).

In the example above we assumed that *A*'s assets (other than cash) were shown in the balance sheet at their saleable value. In practice this will not necessarily be the case. Various methods of valuation might be used and a choice has to be made of the convention to be adopted. For example, we can use the original cost of an asset – its *historical cost*; or we can estimate the value it would realize if it were sold – its *net realizable value*; or we can estimate the cost of replacing it – its *replacement cost*; or we can estimate the *deprival value* – the minimum amount that would just compensate the owner if the asset were destroyed or taken away. We should expect the choice to depend upon the use that is to be made of the accounting statements.

As an example, let us suppose that an individual, *B*, who keeps no accounts, is suspected by the Inspector of Taxes of failing to report all his income. The Inspector may well attempt to estimate *B*'s taxable income over a given year by drawing up balance sheets of *B*'s known or estimated assets and liabilities at the beginning and end of the year and assuming that the difference between the ownership interests or capitals in the two balance sheets, *plus* an estimate of *B*'s personal consumption in the same year, is the income to be taxed. In so doing, the Inspector will, however, wish to exclude changes in the value of *B*'s home, because such changes are not taxable. He can achieve this by leaving the house in both balance sheets at its cost. So here the valuation method is influenced by the tax law.

The group of conventions for valuation and profit measurement known collectively as *historical cost accounting* have been in world-wide use for many years for reporting to owners and shareholders of businesses, and are those assumed in most of this book. The techniques used by accountants to collect and classify financial information are not, however, affected by the particular conventions of valuation and profit measurement adopted. The same techniques can be used equally readily for current value or current cost accounting (discussed in Chapter 12), the introduction of which in place of, or as a supplement to, historical cost accounting is now under active discussion in a number of countries.

3 Business accounts – 1

Business transactions

We shall now apply the ideas of Chapter 2 to business transactions. Our first example will be a small retail business. We shall assume it is managed by the owner, who rents the shop and employs one assistant. Our aim will be to summarize the financial position of the business at various times, and to analyse the transactions leading to changes in this position. The accounting statements will relate to the business only: they will exclude the owner's private affairs, and any other business activities that he carries on. This is an important point: the set of activities covered by accounting statements – sometimes called the *accounting entity* – should always be clearly defined.

We shall record one week's transactions, from one Saturday night to the following Saturday night.* The opening figures which show the business's financial position at the beginning of the period, and the transactions during the period, are set out below. We attach £ signs to indicate that the figures relate to money amounts. Here, as elsewhere in this book, £ signs can be taken to represent multiples of £1 where 'realism' demands it.

Opening figures, showing position on the first Saturday night

	£
Stock of goods for sale ('stock' or 'stock in trade'), valued at the prices at which the goods were originally bought (i.e. at 'historical cost')	100
Owing by customers ('trade debtors') to whom goods have been sold	20
Money in the bank ('cash at bank')	140
Owing to suppliers ('trade creditors') from whom goods have been bought	150
Ownership interest ('capital')	110

* Balance sheets are not usually made up every day – except perhaps, in an approximate way, by banks and similar organizations. But a daily analysis is better for illustration.

Transactions

Monday (*a*) Sold for £25, paid at once, a quantity of stock that originally cost £20; paid the £25 into the bank.

(*b*) Owner withdrew £10 from the bank for personal use. (Such withdrawals from the business by the owner are called *drawings*, unless it is a limited company; then they are called *dividends*.)

Tuesday (*c*) As for (*a*).

(*d*) Paid creditors £150 by sending them cheques drawn on the business bank account.

Wednesday (*e*) As for (*a*).

(*f*) Bought stock costing £160, on one week's credit (i.e. payment is not due to the suppliers until next Tuesday).

(*g*) Bought stock costing £40 for cash (i.e. payment is due at once), payment being by cheque.

Thursday (*h*) As for (*a*).

Friday (*i*) Sold stock that originally cost £40 for £50 in cash, and paid this into the bank.

(*j*) Received the amount owing from the trade debtors, £20, and paid this into the bank.

Saturday (*k*) Sold stock that originally cost £36 for £45 in cash and paid this into the bank.

(*l*) Sold stock that originally cost £24 for £30, on one week's credit.

(*m*) Paid one week's rent of the shop, £10, by cheque.

(*n*) Paid the assistant's weekly wages, £12, by cheque.

The first step in the analysis is to put the opening figures into balance sheet form. We have, first, three classes of assets:

	£
Stock	100
Trade debtors	20
Cash at bank	140
	260

We have one class of non-ownership claims or liabilities:

Trade creditors   £150

It follows that the trader's ownership interest is the difference, £110. We shall not use the term 'wealth' as an alternative to ownership interest, for we are now only concerned with that part of the owner's wealth that relates to this business; his private wealth, and any interests in other businesses, are excluded. The 'ownership interest' can be interpreted as the claim that the owner – now distinct from the business organization – has on the business. It is what the business, as it were, 'owes him', when it is regarded as a separate entity. This is sometimes called the 'capital' of the business. When the business is under the control of a manager who runs it on behalf of the owner, the ownership interest can also be regarded as the recorded value of the economic resources entrusted to the manager by the owner at the date of the balance sheet.

The position at the close of business on the first Saturday night is summarized in balance sheet form in the first column of Table 3.1.

Table 3.1 *Balance sheets*

	£						
	Sat	Mon	Tues	Wed	Thurs	Fri	Sat
Assets							
Stock	100	80	60	240	220	180	120
Trade debtors	20	20	20	20	20	–	30
Cash at bank	140	155	30	15	40	110	133
Total assets	260	255	110	275	280	290	283
Finance							
Trade creditors	150	150	–	160	160	160	160
Ownership interest:							
At beginning of week	110	100	100	100	100	100	100
Profit during week	–	5	10	15	20	30	23
Total ownership interest	110	105	110	115	120	130	123
Total finance	260	255	110	275	280	290	283

The net changes from day to day, and for the whole week, can be summarized conveniently in funds statements for each day, and for the week as a whole. These are shown in Table 3.2. They give us a clear and systematic picture of the changes in the structure of assets and finance during the week.

It will be instructive to work through the transactions, noting how the changes in the balance sheet arise.

Table 3.2 *Funds statements*

	£						
	Sat–Mon	Mon–Tues	Tues–Wed	Wed–Thurs	Thurs–Fri	Fri–Sat	Week
Stock	−20	−20	+180	−20	−40	−60	+20
Trade debtors	–	–	–	–	−20	+30	+10
Cash at bank	+15	−125	−15	+25	+70	+23	−7
	−5	−145	+165	+5	+10	−7	+23
Trade creditors	–	−150	+160	–	–	–	+10
Ownership interest							
At beginning of week	−10	–	–	–	–	–	−10
Profit during week	+5	+5	+5	+5	+10	−7	+23
	−5	−145	+165	+5	+10	−7	+23

We start with transaction (*a*) on Monday. This causes an asset, stock, to be reduced by £20. At the same time another asset, cash at bank, rises by £25. The difference is profit: we have sold for £25 something previously valued in the balance sheet at £20. What we call the *net assets* of the business – assets *less* liabilities to outsiders – have risen by £5. The business, as it were, owes the owner £5 more. This is recorded in a separate line in the table in order to isolate and draw attention to the result of the business transactions for the week.

We can see that the amount of profit recorded depends upon (1) the amount received (or receivable) for the goods sold, and (2) the balance sheet value set upon the stock just before it is sold. As the stock originally cost £20 and was sold for £25 it can be assumed that the business operations have raised its realizable value by the difference. It might seem reasonable, if the sale was confidently expected, to increase the value of the stock and record the profit *before* it was sold. The normal historical cost accounting convention, however, is to follow the procedure shown in the table: gain in value is not acknowledged in the balance sheet until an actual sale provides external evidence of the increased value of the stock. (This statement needs modification, as we shall see in Chapter 12, where a current cost convention is used.)

This illustrates the fact that balance sheets can, at best, only present approximations to economic reality. Conventions are always necessary for at least two reasons. First, personal opinions normally play an important part in valuations: it must not be assumed that there is always a unique valuation figure. Secondly, the everyday routine of accounting calls for clearly defined rules of valuation which will convey a reasonable amount of information and can be applied without undue uncertainty. We shall return to this question later, noting here the practical conclusion that for some purposes the figures in accounts must be regarded only as a kind of approximate memorandum of values or changes in values, and must be interpreted before they are used as a basis for decisions.

We now return to our analysis. The second transaction on Monday (*b*) represents a fall in an asset, cash, and an equivalent fall in the ownership interest: the business has, as it were, satisfied part of this claim by sacrificing cash to the owner. Here the ownership claim changes, but this is *not* due to profit or loss. Drawings can be made by the owner arbitrarily, at any time. So including them as a business expense in calculating the profit would damage the usefulness of the profit figure as an indicator of the business results.

The net effect of the two transactions on Monday appears in the first column of Table 3.2. When the figures in this column are applied to the appropriate figures in the first column of Table 3.1 we obtain the second column of Table 3.1. Readers should check that this is true.

The first transaction on Tuesday (*c*) is a repetition of (*a*). Transaction (*d*), however, is of a new type. It represents a change in balance sheet structure, but does not affect the ownership claim. Creditors have been paid and cash sacrificed in the process: we have a fall in *outside* claims against the business and a fall in assets. In transaction (*a*), on the other hand, there was both a change in asset structure – stock into cash – *and* a net increase in the *ownership* claim.

The net effect of Tuesday's transactions is a fall in assets of £145, a fall in outside claims of £150, and an increase in the ownership claim by £5, as Table 3.2 shows.

On Wednesday we have first a repetition, in (*e*), of Monday's transaction (*a*). Then (*f*), an additional asset, stock, is acquired in exchange for acceptance of a liability – that is, of an outside claim against the business – of £160. We value the stock at the same figure, so that assets and outside claims both rise by £160. A further addition to stock is made (*g*), the consideration being an immediate cash payment of £40. Thus in one case additional assets are acquired by accepting additional claims against the business: that is, the immediate finance is provided from outside the business; in the other case the business itself, by sacrificing cash, provides the finance internally. The flow of funds statement for Wednesday in Table 3.2 brings out the net effect of the three transactions: the information that has required a paragraph of writing appears in the table in a form that can be understood and absorbed at a single glance.

Thursday's transaction (*h*) is again a repetition of (*a*). It appears in the fourth column of Table 3.2.

On Friday there is a transaction (*i*), similar to (*a*) but involving a larger sum: the end of the week is bringing increasing activity. On the same day, trade debtors amounting to £20 are replaced by cash: this is another balance sheet structure change that does not affect profit. Its effect is, however, to make the business more liquid, as it is said: cash can be spent at once; the amount owing in the form of trade debts cannot be spent until it is collected.*

Any change in the structure of assets and liabilities of a business, whether or not there is also a change in the ownership interest, may alter the liquidity of the business, that is, may affect the cash it holds or its ability to obtain cash in the sense that it may change (1) the speed with which it can obtain a given cash sum, and (2) the amount of asset value it must sacrifice, if any, in order to obtain the cash sooner rather than later. Thus, transaction (*i*), in which stock was sold for cash, represented *both* a profitable transaction *and* a movement towards increased liquidity.†

The net effect of Friday's transactions appears in the fifth column of Table 3.2.

On Saturday we have, first, a sales transaction (*k*) like (*a*). Next there is another sales transaction (*l*), in which a debt is accepted instead of cash in exchange for the stock. In business language, (*k*) is called a *cash sale*, (*l*) a *credit sale*; in both cases there is a fall in an asset (stock), a rise in another asset (in one case cash, in the other trade debtors), and a rise in the ownership interest (profit). Next we have two transactions, (*m*) and (*n*), in each of which there is a fall in an asset (cash) but no corresponding increase in another asset and no fall in a liability. Instead there is, in both cases, a fall in the ownership

---

* It is sometimes possible to sell debts to a third party, or borrow on the security of debts, before they are due, thus securing cash quickly, but in such cases a sacrifice of part of the value of the debt has to be made – i.e. as 'discount' or 'interest' – as the price of this.

† If the stock had been sold quickly in order to obtain increased liquidity, it might have been necessary to accept a lower price (and therefore lower profit) than if it was sold more slowly.

interest. These falls are not due to withdrawal of money value from the business by the owner, as in (*b*): they are incurred as part of the process of running the business. They are an offset against the profit and are called *expenses*. Thus, unlike drawings, which transfer value to the owner, expenses reduce the profit: the amounts in question have been spent in the course of the business activity. The ownership interest is thereby reduced, though no doubt in the hope that the sum of such sacrifices in any period will be more than offset by the profit margin earned by the sales.*

Saturday's transactions are summarized in the sixth column of Table 3.2. The final column summarizes the transactions for the week. If we rearrange this for presentation as a weekly report to the owner we have a statement on the lines of Table 3.3. We see that sources of funds are *increases in claims or decreases in assets*: uses of funds are *increases in assets or decreases in claims*. A fall in cash can

Table 3.3 *Funds statement for week ending* ——

	£
Sources of funds	
Profit for week	23
Drawings	10
Profit retained in the business	13
Increase in finance from creditors	10
	23
Uses of funds	
Increase in investment in stock	20
Increase in finance absorbed by debtors	10
	30
Net decrease in cash at bank	7

* As we shall see later, some outlays of this kind are assumed to create an asset of equivalent value. It is to some extent a matter of convention, merely affecting the time when profits and losses are recorded, what payments are assumed to give rise to immediate profit reductions (expenses) and what are considered to create equivalent assets, as when stock is bought. If payments like wages are treated as if they raised the value of stock by an equivalent amount, the recorded profit is then not reduced by the amount of the payment at the moment of the outlay; but the profit shown at the moment when the stock is sold is at the time of sale correspondingly smaller, as the recorded value of the stock at the time of sale is higher.

be regarded as a source, but because of its special importance some people prefer to show it, as in Table 3.3, as the net result of other sources and uses.

We can, by extracting figures from the set of flows for the week, and expanding them by reference to the original data, obtain two other statements of particular importance. Row 3 of Table 3.2 yields, when expanded, a detailed cash statement (Table 3.4). The balance at the bank at the end of the week, as shown in Table 3.1, is also inserted. Statements of this kind are an important part of the financial control and keep management informed of the cash position of the business and of reasons for its change. Prepared as forecasts or budgets they are a central tool of management planning.

Table 3.4 *Cash statement for week ending* ——

	£
Receipts	
Cash sales	195
Debtors	20
	215
Payments	
Cash purchases	40
Creditors	150
Expenses	22
Drawings	10
	222
Net change	−7
Balance at bank at end of week	133

Row 7 of Table 3.2, when expanded and summarized, provides a detailed *profit and loss statement* for the week (Table 3.5).

In ordinary language, Table 3.5 tells us that sales revenue *less* the cost of sales (the difference being the *gross profit* or *gross margin*) is, for the week, £45; that £10 was spent on rent and £12 on wages, so that the expenses of the business for the week amounted to £22; and that the net profit, or gain in value of the ownership claim, *so far as this was due to business transactions*, was therefore £23. The qualification is necessary, as there was a fall of £10 in the ownership interest between Saturday and Monday when the owner drew £10 from the

Table 3.5 *Profit and loss statement for week ending* ——

	£	
Sales		225
Cost of sales		180
Gross profit		45
Expenses		
Rent	10	
Wages	12	22
Profit		23

business: as noted already *such transactions are not relevant for the profit and loss analysis*. The withdrawal of money, or the payment of money into the business, by the owner, belong to a class of transactions with a different economic significance. This is so whether the withdrawal is regarded as a withdrawal of value the owner has previously paid into the business (that is, of 'capital'), or of profit subsequently earned. The distinction between the earning of profit and the use that is made of that profit is important and is sometimes indicated by describing the use as an *appropriation* of profit, and the statement recording it as an *appropriation account*.

The words 'cost of sales' as they are used here have a technical meaning: the figure to which they refer is the cost of buying the goods that have been sold and, in relation to any particular lot of goods, measures the value at which they are entered in the balance sheet before they are sold. The total cost of goods is not the whole cost incurred by the business during the period. It excludes such expenses as the rent and wages in this example, which, nevertheless, the business must incur in order to be able to buy and sell goods. It is convenient to classify cost of sales separately, because of its special significance as an expense the level of which tends to vary in direct proportion to the value of the goods sold; this is less likely to be true of other expenses. Later we shall see that the term is also used in manufacturing businesses, though with a somewhat different significance.

Finance from retained profit

The reader will notice that if the owner withdraws money from the business there is no economic criterion by which one can say whether he is withdrawing part of his original capital or part of any profit that has been earned; he is withdrawing an asset, and, as a result, the net ownership claim is reduced; the allocation of the withdrawal to the capital or to the profit part of the ownership interest is a matter of convention.

Another point to be noted is that profit earned is not the same as money received. The study of the tables above should make it clear that profit measurement is related to changes in the recorded value of *all* the assets, *less* the liabilities, taken together. Hence a profit can arise in a period when the holding of money (cash) has *fallen*. This indeed has happened in our example. The final column of Table 3.2 shows that, though the profit is £23, cash has fallen by £7. The net increase over the week in what is called *working capital*, that is, cash, trade debtors and stock, *less* trade creditors, all taken together, is only £13: this is £10 less than the profit. The difference is due to the withdrawal of £10 by the proprietor. Notice that leaving profit in the business is equivalent to providing extra ownership finance: the additional ownership claim finances the net increase in assets which gave rise to it. As soon as the profit arises the owner can be said to provide extra finance equal to that profit: he is from that time on exercising his right of choice not to withdraw assets from the business equivalent to the amount of the profit.

In Chapter 4 we shall show how the figures for the statements described in this chapter emerge from the *double entry book-keeping system* in which they are classified and summarized.

4 Double entry book-keeping

We have seen how accounting statements can be used to summarize financial data in a convenient form. However, a systematic way of collecting and classifying the extensive original data is also required. This is provided by the *double entry system of book-keeping*.* In its essentials the system consists of a set of statistical tables or *ledger accounts*,† one for each class of asset or claim. The figures in each such table are so arranged as to form a continuous record of the value initially recorded and the subsequent changes in value. Furthermore, in order to facilitate arithmetical control, a system of recording is used which in essence amounts to treating assets and claims as of opposite algebraic sign.

The fundamental ideas of the system are illustrated in Table 4.1. In this table the original numerical information from the example in Chapter 3 is analysed into the appropriate balance sheet classifications. There is a column for each type of asset and for each type of claim: these columns are the ledger accounts; they are numbered from (1) to (6). Each ledger account has a left-hand side (which we may call the + side) and a right-hand side (which we may call the − side). These are also called, respectively, the *debit* and the *credit* sides, and we shall henceforth use these traditional terms (which are written for short as *dr* and *cr*). It is important to realize that the terms 'debit' and 'credit' as they are used in accounting have a purely technical meaning. The reader should put out of his mind firmly any previous conception that debit necessarily implies loss and that credit necessarily implies gain. The accounting meaning of these terms is given in the statement of the rules of the double entry system in the next paragraph. This statement is a *definition* of debit and credit: it

---

* The traditional word 'book-keeping' now includes recording by mechanical and electronic means.

† The term 'ledger account' is derived from the traditional ledger or book in which double entry accounts were kept. The name no longer implies the existence of a book, only of a systematic collection of numerical records.

is from the statement that the terms derive their meaning in this book.

The fundamental rules of the double entry system are as follows:

Assets and *increases in assets* are entered as *left-hand side* or *positive* (+) items and are called *debits*.

Claims and *increases in claims* are entered as *right-hand side* or *negative* (−) items and are called *credits*.

Decreases in assets are entered as *right-hand side* or *negative* (−) items and are called *credits*.

Decreases in claims are entered as *left-hand side* or *positive* (+) items and are called *debits*.

It follows from the definition of assets and claims that any change in one account must always be accompanied by a change of opposite sign in another account or, to use the traditional language, *every debit has its credit*.*

Thus we may have:

An increase in an asset (debit) accompanied by:
    (*a*) an equal increase in a claim (credit), *or*
    (*b*) an equal decrease in another asset (credit).
An increase in a claim (credit) accompanied by:
    (*a*) an equal increase in an asset (debit), *or*
    (*b*) an equal decrease in another claim (debit).
A decrease in an asset (credit) accompanied by:
    (*a*) an equal decrease in a claim (debit), *or*
    (*b*) an equal increase in another asset (debit).
A decrease in a claim (debit) accompanied by:
    (*a*) an equal decrease in an asset (credit), *or*
    (*b*) an equal increase in another claim (credit).

These rules are invariable. It should be noted, however, that in practice it is often convenient, when recording items, to merge more than one entry together, so that, for example, one debit entry may be matched by several credit entries which sum to the same amount; and so on.

Let us apply these rules in Table 4.1. In Column (1) we have, on the first line, the stock at the beginning of the period, the *opening balance*. This is £100, the balance sheet value at that time. The first transaction (*a*) is the sale of stock, valued at £20, for £25. This can be regarded, for balance sheet analysis, as a combination of two

---

* The opposite side of a given entry – the debit corresponding to a given credit or vice versa – is sometimes called the *contra* entry or simply 'the contra'.

B

Table 4.1 *Double entry analysis*

Asset increases and claim decreases (debits) appear on the left-hand side of accounts. Claim increases and asset decreases (credits) appear on the right-hand side of accounts.

	(1) Stock		(2) Trade debtors		(3) Cash at bank		(4) Trade creditors		(5) Capital		(6) Profit and loss	
	Dr +£	Cr −£	Dr +£	Cr −£	Dr +£	Cr −£	Dr +£	Cr −£	Dr +£	Cr −£	Dr +£	Cr −£
Opening balances	100		20		140			150		110		
Monday												
(a)		20			25							5
(b)						10			10			
Tuesday												
(c)		20			25							5
(d)						150	150					
Wednesday												
(e)		20			25							5
(f)	160							160				
(g)	40					40						
Thursday												
(h)		20			25							5
Friday												
(i)		40			50							10
(j)				20	20							
Saturday												
(k)		36			45							9
(l)		24	30									6
(m)						10					10	
(n)						12					12	
	300	180	50	20	355	222	150	310	10	110	22	45
Closing balances*	120		30		133			160		100		23

* Net differences between debit and credit items. If the debit total is greater than the credit total in any column, the balance must appear on the debit side; and contrariwise, if the credit total is the greater. The closing balances of one period are the opening balances of the next.

transactions. The first is the conversion of £20 of asset value in stock into another asset, cash. The second is an addition of £5 to asset value (cash) with an equal increase in the ownership interest (profit). The reduction of £20 in stock is entered on the credit side of the stock account. The second part of the double entry is a corresponding debit of £20 in the cash account in Column (3), for the increase in cash; this is not shown separately, but appears as part of a cash receipt of £25. The remaining £5 of the latter is the debit corresponding to a £5 credit in the profit and loss account (Column 6): this is the profit margin and represents an increase in the ownership claim. We have, in effect, two pairs of debits and credits: the two debits, both to the cash account, sum to £25 and are shown as one item; the two credits, one to stock account and one to the profit and loss account, similarly sum to £25.

At the close of business on Monday the sums of the items on the two sides of the stock account are £100 and £20, the debit side being greater than the credit side. The arithmetical difference is £80. This difference is called a *debit balance* of £80. A balance must always be given a sign: that is, it must be described as debit or credit. If we wished, we could draw a line across the account at this point (as at the bottom of the table) and start again with a fresh opening balance of £80 on the debit side and nothing on the credit side.

The significance of the remaining items in the stock account can be analysed in the same way. The final line of this account shows £120 as the debit balance at the end of the period: this closing balance is the balance sheet value of stock at that date, and is the opening balance of the next period.

The next column (2) is the trade debtors account.* We start with the balance sheet value at the beginning of the period: this is the opening debit balance, £20. This remains unchanged until Friday, when the debts are paid (*j*). The asset then falls by £20: in other words there is a credit entry of £20, reducing the balance of the account to zero. The corresponding debit is found in the cash account in Column (3): the decrease in the asset 'debtors' (a credit) has been offset by an increase in the asset 'cash' (a debit).

On Saturday more debts are acquired, amounting to £30, and there is a debit entry of this amount (*l*). This is the sum of £24 (the other side of the transaction being the fall in stock in Column (1)) and £6 (the other side being a rise in profit in Column (6)).

There are no more items in this account; the closing balance of the trade debtors account is therefore £30 debit.

The changes in the cash account can be similarly analysed.

Ledger account (4) is concerned, not with a class of assets, but with trade creditors, a class of claims. The opening balance is £150, and being a claim on the business this is a credit, or negative, balance. This is unchanged until Tuesday. On that day the creditors are paid (*d*). The creditors balance is then reduced by £150 and the cash balance falls by the same amount: reduction in a claim is

* 'Trade debtors' is here used as an adjective qualifying 'account': hence we do not use an apostrophe after the final *s* of debtors.

accompanied by reduction in an asset. The balance of trade creditors is now zero. On Wednesday fresh claims are incurred, of £160 (*f*). This requires a credit entry, and there is a corresponding debit entry in the stock account recording the increase in stock.

There are no more changes in the trade creditors account, the final balance of which is therefore £160 credit.

We now come to ledger accounts (5) and (6). These, too, are concerned with a claim. This claim, however, is not in respect of a liability, as was the claim of Column (4); we are now concerned with the ownership interest. It is important to maintain this distinction, for although the double entry rules for both types of claim are the same the financial significance is different.* In order to analyse separately the business results, the ownership claim is divided into two accounts, one showing the ownership interest at the beginning of the week and the ownership drawings during the week, and the other containing the profit analysis. This division corresponds to the division in the balance sheets in Table 3.1. The first account we call the *capital account* (Column 5) and the second the *profit and loss account* (Column 6).

The opening balance of the capital account shows the ownership claim at the beginning of the week, £110. This is a credit. On Monday this claim is reduced by £10 when the owner withdraws cash (*b*). This requires a debit entry, reducing the balance to £100. The contra entry is the credit of £10 in the cash account. No other transactions between owner and business occur during the week, and we end with a credit balance of £100. (The next step might be to re-classify as capital the profit of £23 for the week, shown in Column (6), before starting the next week, in order to show the total ownership interest at the beginning of that week. This step is not shown here; it will be introduced in later examples.)

Finally we have the profit and loss account in Column (6). This account has no opening balance, as the whole ownership interest at the beginning of the week was classified as capital. On Monday there is a profit of £5, corresponding, as we have already seen, to £5 out of the increase of £25 in cash which occurs that day (*a*). The profit of £5 is therefore recorded as a credit entry in the profit and loss account. This entry is followed by a series of similar ones.

On Saturday two reductions in profit are recorded in the account as debits. These are expenses, the contra items to the cash payments

* Ledger accounts concerned with the ownership claim are sometimes called *nominal accounts*.

for rent and wages. We thus have two debits for £10 and £12 respectively.

The credit side of the profit and loss account totals £45. The debit side totals £22. The balance at the end of the period is therefore £23 credit. As there was no opening balance this is a measure of the net profit made by the business during the week: the owner's claim on the business has risen by £23 as a result – the business 'owes' him £23 more, as it were. This reflects the additional net assets recorded.

Let us recapitulate. The balance sheet, and the detailed double entry records from which it is in practice extracted, can be regarded as a statement of:

1 the resources that have been put into the hands of the management of the business, the assets; and
2 the claims of the persons to whom the top management is responsible for these assets, of which the claim of the owner or owners has a special and quite distinct significance.

The claims always equal the assets because what would otherwise be an excess of assets over liabilities is always balanced exactly by the ownership claim for the residue. It is normally one of the jobs of the management to produce profit; but as soon as it has been produced there is an increase in the management responsibility because of the additional net resources now in its hands.*

The numerical sum of the debits in a double entry system must always equal the numerical sum of the credits; this follows from our definitions and is an expression of the fact that the respective totals of asset values and claims are always equal. A balance sheet can always be extracted from the double entry records by listing all the balances, debit and credit, as they are at a given point of time.† If we think in terms of algebraic sign, we can say that the algebraic sum of the asset values and the claims must always be zero. If this is found in practice not to be so, we know there is an error in the records.

It has been traditional in book-keeping to use the left-hand and right-hand side convention illustrated in Table 4.1. This convention remains a valuable practical method of classification, and is one that

* When we look at a business which is managed by its owner, we have to distinguish the latter's economic function as manager of the business from his function as owner: he is, so to speak, responsible to himself in another function.

† Entries in the double entry records must therefore always be dated, directly or by some system of coding.

all accountants use as a matter of course when they think and write. However, it is often convenient, in the practical work of collecting and classifying data, to work in terms of plus and minus, particularly where mechanical or electronic devices are in use. The terms 'debit' and 'credit' are always retained as well, however.*

It is important to note, in order to avoid possible confusion, that the left-hand and right-hand side convention for indicating debits and credits, and the plus and minus interpretation that we have given here, are not, in general, used in the presentation of reports. Thus balance sheets do not necessarily follow the 'left hand for debits' and 'right hand for credits' rule. The profit and loss report to shareholders is sometimes in a more or less conventional double entry form; but it is more likely to be in some other form. In short it is essential to distinguish between the techniques and symbols used in collecting and classifying the data and those used in preparing reports, based on the same data.†

The full description of any given ledger account includes the word 'account': thus we have cash account, capital account, stock account, and so on. However, it is often convenient to drop the second word and speak simply of cash, capital, stock, etc., when it is clear that we are referring to the ledger accounts.

If he has not already done so, the reader is advised at this stage to work carefully through the figures we have been discussing. He should start with the data given at the beginning of Chapter 3 and check each opening balance and each transaction against the figures in Table 4.1, noting as he does this the relationship between the classified analysis for each day in Table 4.1 and the flow of funds for each day in Table 3.2. Finally he should check the last row of Table 4.1 with the final column of Table 3.1. Once these relationships have been grasped the transition to more complicated problems of

---

* The algebraic signs could be reversed, since which is + and which is − is a convention. The essential point to remember is that debits and credits have opposite algebraic signs. Debit and credit are written for short *dr* and *cr*, as already indicated. A useful way of remembering which side is debit and which credit is to note that 'credit' contains the letter *r* for *right*-hand side.

† Reports often show that a particular figure is negative by enclosing it in brackets, so that (300) for example means that the 300 must be deducted from the numbers without brackets with which it is associated. The nature of the latter will determine whether such a negative is a credit or a debit: this must be judged from the context.

double entry book-keeping should not cause much difficulty. A modern accounting system is essentially a routine for collecting a very large number of pieces of original information, sorting these out, classifying them, and then recording them in a set of ledger accounts that in essence, though not in detail, are like those in Table 4.1. From these can be prepared statements, among others, of the same type as those in Tables 3.1 to 3.5.

Debit and credit

In accounting the terms 'debit' and 'credit' have a specific, technical meaning. Unfortunately these terms are also used in everyday speech in a looser and more general way. In consequence it is not always easy, in the early stages of the study of accounting, to avoid some confusion of thought. For example, it may not be easy for a reader to appreciate why he should, when he receives a prize of £50 on his premium bonds, be expected to *debit* his cash account. He feels that a credit would be more appropriate, since he associates the word credit with gain, and debit with loss.

In fact, the popular use of the word 'credit' in this context contains, from an accountant's viewpoint, only half the truth. In order to understand the accounting we must analyse the significance of the cash receipt in balance sheet terms. The recipient of the prize has experienced an increase in a certain class of asset, cash. His personal balance sheet therefore shows an increase of £50 in his assets. If there is no other change in his balance sheet, it will no longer balance, however: assets will exceed claims. This is impossible; in fact we say that the increase in assets has resulted in an equal increase in claims on assets – an increase in capital. When this is recorded the balance sheet is once more in balance.

Thus, the recipient, if he keeps his accounts by double entry, *credits* his capital account, as a record of the increase in his total wealth (which may be regarded as an increase in the money value of the total claim on resources capable of being satisfied out of the assets he holds). He also records the increase in the asset cash, and this requires a *debit* in the cash account. The transaction requires both a credit *and* a debit, for both parts of the balance sheet are affected, claims as well as assets.

For those who find it easier to visualize matters of this kind in personal terms, we can illustrate debit and credit in another and older way. To do this we go back to a method used in book-keeping treatises of the sixteenth century that still has significance in relation to the control of assets in modern accounting systems. Let us suppose that the name of each ledger account stood for a person who at any given point of time either *owed* money (or something of value in terms of money) *to* the business whose accounts we were handling, or was *owed* money or money value *by* it. When 'cash' took the form of gold or other coin in the box or chest, we should have thought of the cash account as the account of a person who received cash for the business, looked after it, made payments on its behalf, and was responsible to it for the balance. The cash account reflected the money entrusted to him – the *cashier* – and could be regarded as a kind of debtors account. If we had thought in this way it would have seemed quite sensible to *debit* cash account when the business received cash: the cash account (or the cashier, for whom it stood) 'owed' this money to the business. (Indeed we still sometimes talk of a 'charge' to an account instead of a 'debit'.) When the cashier paid money out, the account was credited, for he had now 'discharged' his responsibility: a cash payment was therefore a *credit* to the cash account. The debit balance on the cash account showed the amount the cashier had received and had not yet spent: it is what he should have had in the cash box – and this could be checked by counting. The fact that in some circumstances the cashier might also have been the owner of the business need not affect our reasoning: the cash account was concerned with the *function* of holding money. Nowadays money received is usually paid at once into the bank, so we *debit* the bank, which now owes the money (we may call the account 'cash at bank'); and we *credit* the bank when it pays out money for the business.*

We can look on other asset accounts in a similar way. Thus a debit of £1,000 to the account for motor vehicles can be regarded as recording the receipt of £1,000 of value, in the form of the vehicles, by the person responsible for these; and if we reduce the recorded value of these, e.g. because they are partly worn out, we credit the account because value has been given up: the responsibility has been reduced.

It is easy to see that accounts of creditors can be looked at in the

---

* The term 'cash' is now used when it would be more appropriate to speak of 'bank'; in the text we have used 'cash at bank' where it has seemed necessary to avoid ambiguity. Coin and notes actually held by the cashier for small payments are now called 'petty cash'. Money in his hands awaiting payment into the bank is usually recorded as if already paid in, i.e. as a debit to the bank.

same way. When someone lends us money we *credit* him because he has given up value to us (cash or bank being debited); and when we repay him we *debit* him because he has received value from us (cash or bank being credited).

Finally, we can look on the accounts for the owner or owners as recording the amount 'owed' to the owner by the business. These accounts comprise the capital account, the profit and loss account, and sub-divisions of the latter (*revenue* and *expense* accounts which we shall discuss later). These accounts taken together show the ownership interest (or claim) and changes in this. When there is a net rise in this (e.g. as the result of a sale of an asset at a profit) we can say the owner is immediately owed more by the business: he can therefore be said in a sense to 'give' value to the business, and he must be *credited* through the profit and loss account. Similarly if the owner pays in money, we *debit* cash (the bank has received it) and we *credit* the owner. If the owner withdraws cash, we *debit* him for now he is 'owed' less: he has received value. If a loss is made (e.g. a cash payment is made for which no value is received), the owner is immediately owed less by the business, and we *debit* him – in the first instance in the profit and loss account or in one of the sections of this which we call expense accounts.

Thus we can derive the following alternative formulation of our general rule for the use of debit and credit:

Debit the account that represents the recipient of value.
Credit the account that represents the giver of value.

In interpreting this rule we must remember, however, that the owner has usually a number of accounts, the balances on which together make up the total of his interest; that a fall in total owner-ship value (which may be a loss) is interpreted as a receipt of value by the owner in the sense that the business thereby 'owes' him less; and that a rise in ownership value (which may be a profit) is inter-preted as a giving of value by the owner, the business thenceforth 'owing' him more.

If value is received by one person, it must be given by another. Hence every transaction must have both a debit and a credit aspect.

This formulation can be illustrated by applying it to the first four transactions in the example in Table 4.1 (overleaf).

If the results of a transaction are regarded in this light, it becomes natural to write, for example, as a summary of transaction (*a*) above, 'Bank is debtor to stock and profit, £25'. This type of statement is

Trans-action	Debit, for value received		Credit, for value given	
		£		£
(a)	Bank	25	Stock	20
			Owner (profit and loss account)	5
(b)	Owner (capital account)	10	Bank	10
(c)	Bank	25	Stock	20
			Owner (profit and loss account)	5
(d)	Creditors	150	Bank	150

typical of early book-keeping, and still survives, e.g. in such documents as bills rendered for goods and services, which often read: '*A* debtor to *B*, for goods supplied, £25', and so on. (This explains the contraction *dr* for debit.)

In the past, ledger accounts have sometimes been divided into *real accounts*, *personal accounts*, and *nominal accounts*, according to whether they refer to things (e.g. stock), persons (e.g. debtors) or ownership (e.g. capital or profit).

Any reader who would like to know more about the early history of book-keeping will find much to interest him in the collection of essays by Littleton and Yamey (mentioned in the reading list at the end of the book). The study of some of these essays can be an active help in learning the rules of double entry, in that they show how the present-day conventions arose.

Ledger accounts

In Table 4.1 we set out the ledger accounts in columns in such a way that the correspondence between the debit and credit entries for each particular transaction could be easily seen and checked. Later we shall adopt a more flexible practice, writing down the accounts in any order and position that we find convenient. In this we shall be following business practice: any double entry system must consist of a set of ledger accounts, but the precise form they take, and their location, is a matter of choice. When we do this we shall use the 'T account' form (so called from the practice of ruling a line along the top of the account and another down the middle to divide the debit and credit sides, thus forming a kind of T).

Suppose we have the following cash transactions:

favourable opening balance at bank   £25
received from debtors   £30
paid to creditors   £25
paid as wages   £26
paid as rent   £8

The cash account in T form would have appeared as follows:

Cash at bank

	£		£
Balance	25	Creditors	25
Debtors	30	Wages	26
		Rent	8
	—		—
	55		59
		Balance	4

Notice that, as credits exceed debits, the final balance is 'unfavourable', i.e. is an amount owed *to* the bank.

This form is based on the traditional double entry ledger that was used in the Italian city-states at least as early as the fourteenth century,[*] though some of the historical trimmings have been dropped.[†] It provides a standard form for summarizing transactions, and for distinguishing clearly and quickly between debit and credit items when the logic of a particular transaction is being analysed.

An alternative form is often used, e.g. by accounting machines and computer print-outs, in which an additional column allows the balance to be recorded after each transaction, without entering totals, as follows:

Cash at bank

	Dr	Cr	Balance
Balance			25 dr
Debtors	30		55 dr
Creditors		25	30 dr
Wages		26	4 dr
Rent		8	4 cr
Balance			4 cr

[*] See A. C. Littleton and B. S. Yamey, *Studies in the History of Accounting* (London, 1956).

[†] For example, the words 'to' and 'by', preceding debit and credit entries respectively, have been omitted.

Here the balance column is not part of the double entry. Note that it is necessary to indicate whether the figure in the balance column is a debit or a credit balance, since this is not indicated by its position, as in the T account.

There is an alternative way of recording balances in the T form of account. A purist could argue that to insert a balance in a ledger account as a new figure, after ruling off the debit and credit columns, is to violate the rule that every debit entry must be accompanied by a credit entry, since the new balance is only entered once. This objection is dealt with by inserting the new balance twice, once on each side. Thus, in the cash account given below, the new balance of £4 is inserted on the credit side, as we have it, but the same figure is also inserted on the side with the smaller total *above* the ruling (so that it does not affect the new total). Both totals above the ruling are then necessarily equal, and our cash account appears as follows:

Cash at bank

	£		£
Balance b/d	25	Creditors	25
Debtors	30	Wages	26
Balance c/d	4	Rent	8
	—		—
	59		59
		Balance b/d	4

The balance inserted above the ruling on the side with the smaller total is called the *balance carried down* (c/d for short) and the opening balance in the next period is called the *balance brought down* (b/d). The final result is just the same as before; but the arithmetical accuracy of the new balance is proved visually by the equality of the preceding totals. We can assume that the opening balance of £25 had a corresponding credit in the previous section of the account.

Journal form

It is necessary in practice to set up a systematic and carefully controlled procedure for collecting and classifying original data before it reaches the ledger accounts. We shall have more to say about this later. In earlier days it was customary to summarize the information for each transaction, showing the relevant debits and credits in chronological order in a book called the *journal* which provided a link between the original information and the final ledger entries. The journal was not a formal part of the double entry; but all the double entry records were derived from it. In it the effect of each transaction was set out in a standard form which showed clearly the debits and credits concerned, and included a note or *narrative* explaining the transaction. The journal entry summarized, as it were, the accounting logic of each transaction.

The entry would take the following form:

		£	£
1823			
21 Jan.	J. Brown	dr 100	
	to Sales*		100
	For sale of 20 bags of meal		

This told the book-keeper to debit £100 to Brown's account and to credit £100 to the sales account; as he made the entries in the ledger he would note in the journal the pages (or 'folios') in the ledger where these entries were to be found, and in the ledger the relevant page of the journal. Thus, the completion of the work of writing up the ledger, called *posting* the ledger, would be shown by the presence in the journal of all the ledger page references, and every entry in the ledger could be traced back to its source.

The journal is still used to some extent for unusual transactions that do not fit into the prescribed routines that have replaced it for most purposes. Our concern with it here, however, is with form: the journal form can provide a convenient shorthand description of any book-keeping entry, and is constantly used by accountants for this purpose (usually without the historical trimmings of 'dr' and 'to'). If an accountant writes:

	£	£
Interest on loan	100	
Cash		100

he is describing a transaction, the book-keeping results of which will be to debit the interest account (a sub-section of the profit and loss account) with £100 and to credit the cash account with the same amount. The whole transaction is thus summed up succinctly. Or

* Sales account is a sub-section of the profit and loss account.

suppose that only £60 is to be paid out in cash to the lender immediately, the remaining £40 being paid later to the tax authorities, as in certain situations might be required by law. The tax authorities become creditors for the £40. We show the whole transaction as follows:

	£	£
Interest on loan	100	
Cash		60
Inland Revenue Commissioners		40

5 Form of financial reports

There are three main types of private business enterprise: individuals carrying on business alone, called *sole traders*; individuals in *partnership*; and *limited companies*. Differences in the way in which these are financed, and differences in the way the law affects them, coupled with tradition and habit, have led to differences in the form of their accounting reports. The main difference is in the ownership section.

Sole traders

We have already considered the accounting reports of a sole trader. In Table 3.1 the ownership interest was divided into two parts. The first part showed the capital as it was at the beginning of the week, less the subsequent drawings. The second showed the profit earned during the week. This division was maintained in the funds statement in Table 3.2. Thus the reader was able to distinguish between the ownership interest at the beginning of the period and the net profit earned by the business activities.

In one sense the capital of any business at any time is the whole ownership interest at the beginning of the period, *plus* any profit earned, *less* any withdrawals made by the owner, *plus* any payments the owner has made into the business, up to that time. In this sense the capital shown in Table 3.1 on, say, Wednesday night was £115: the original capital on the first Saturday night, £110, *plus* three days' profit, £15, *less* drawings on Monday, £10. In businesses run by a sole trader the distinction between capital and profit is in fact normally only made for the purposes of each distinct accounting year: the capital at the beginning of each accounting year is distinguished in the balance sheet from the profit of that year, but the two figures (*less* any drawings and *plus* any more capital paid in) are merged at the end of the year. Hence the capital of a sole trader at the beginning of each year is said to be the whole ownership interest at that time.

In this respect sole traders differ from limited companies and, to a lesser extent, partnerships. This difference is reflected in their accounting reports, as we shall see below, and among other things reflects the fact that a sole trader, unlike the shareholders of a limited company, is liable for all the debts of his business.

Partnerships

Two or more persons may carry on a business together in partnership. Such an arrangement implies the existence of a legal agreement (which may or may not be written) about the amount of capital each partner is to contribute and keep in the business, what share of the profits is to go to each, how drawings are to be regulated, and generally how the business is to be run. In order to give effect to the arrangement, the accounting records and balance sheets contain a *capital account* for each partner. What the partner contributes as capital is credited to this account. Sometimes his drawings are debited to this account and his share of the profit transferred to it from the profit and loss account at the end of each accounting period.

More often, perhaps, a distinction is made between the more permanent capital paid in by each partner, shown in his capital account, and his share of profits earned *less* drawings, which are shown in a *current account*. In the latter case, each partner's share of profit is credited to the current account at the end of each accounting period, and his drawings are debited to it as they occur. This distinction between capital account and current account arises from the nature of the contract between the partners: if the partnership agreement requires each partner not to withdraw from the business any amount that would reduce an agreed paid-in capital, the balance sheet must show how much of the ownership claim consists of this agreed capital. Thus in a partnership the word 'capital' can mean the whole ownership interest, or only part of it, according to the context.

Like a sole trader, a partner is personally liable for all the debts of the business.

Limited companies

The typical legal form of business organization in the private sector in industrial countries with market economies is the *limited company* or *business corporation*. In legal theory this is an artificial or fictitious 'person' which is assumed to have many of the same rights and duties as a natural person. The company is in legal form owned by its *shareholders* or *members*, who provide its capital and share in its profits. The company itself is the legal owner of the business assets, and is responsible to the limit of its assets for the liabilities and for any obligations imposed on it by law, such as those to its employees. As it is not a real person it has to be managed by *directors*, appointed for the purpose by the shareholders in general meeting.

The rights and duties of companies, and of shareholders and directors, are regulated by the *company law*.

Capital is paid into companies in the form of units called *shares*, each of which usually has a *par* or *nominal* value, say £1 or 25p. The shares are 'issued' to the shareholders who first contribute money (or sometimes other assets) to the company. A person may own one share or many. The par value distinguishes the minimum amount that must be paid in for each share, though the issue price may be greater than par, in which case the excess is called a *share premium*. Once the issue price of a share is fully paid, no more need be contributed, but until then a legal obligation remains on the person who owns the share to pay up the remainder of the issue price. Shares can be transferred from one person to another: in effect this is a transfer of a parcel of legal rights and obligations. The rules of some companies impose restrictions on this right of transfer: this might happen where the shares were owned by members of the same family, who did not want to admit outsiders as shareholders.

Thus the two most basic characteristics of limited companies, which distinguish them from partnerships, are the limitation of shareholders' liability for the company's debts to the issue price of the shares, and the transferability of individual shares.

It is possible to have more than one *class* of shares, such for example that the holders of one class (usually called *preference shares*) have a prior right to a specified share of profit each year, and a prior right to repayment of capital if the company comes to an end – when it *winds up* or *liquidates*. In such cases the remaining shares, usually called *ordinary shares*, are entitled to the residue or *equity*. Each share in one particular class carries the same rights and obligations as any other share of the same class.

The price to be paid for the limitation of liability and the convenience of transferability is strict regulation by company law. An outstanding feature of company law is its requirements for the provision of information about the company and its activities, both directly to shareholders and others with a financial interest in the company, and indirectly to the public at large through registration of information with a government office – the Companies Registration Office – whose files are open to public inspection.

Many of these requirements of company law relate specifically to the keeping of accounting records and the provision of accounting information. All companies must keep detailed accounting records and must provide annual balance sheets and profit and loss accounts, the form and contents of which comply with legal requirements.

The conventions of asset valuation and profit calculation described in this book have been largely developed in response to the needs of companies. These accounting conventions have strongly influenced those used in other organizations, such as the public corporations that run state industries. So the study of company accounting embraces a large part of financial accounting generally.

Features which distinguish company accounting reports ('company accounts') from those of sole traders and partnerships include:

1   Tax on a company's profits is paid by the company, and is shown in its accounts; whereas tax on the profits of sole traders and partnerships is assessed on the individual persons and does not normally appear in the business accounts.

2   In a company, all shares of a given class are indistinguishable, one from another, as regards rights to dividends, voting in meetings, etc. (once they are fully paid) so that there is no need in the accounts to distinguish individual capital or current accounts of shareholders, as there is in partnerships. (The French name for a company limited by shares – *société anonyme* – recognizes this.)

3   It is a basic rule of company law that the amount of capital subscribed by shareholders shall be recorded and shown separately in the balance sheet as *share capital* and (where the original issue price of shares was greater than their declared nominal value) *share premiums*. This requirement is related to requirements of company law that limit the amounts that can be distributed to the shareholders as dividends, and in particular make it illegal deliberately to return subscribed capital to the shareholders without going through a prescribed legal process, intended to protect creditors. In consequence, that part of the shareholders' interest that arises from profits and from increases in the recorded values of assets are distinguished: in Britain these are collectively called *reserves*.

In Britain a distinction is made between companies which may have large numbers of shareholders and whose shares may be listed on the stock exchange (public companies), and others (private companies). A similar distinction is found in other countries. The accounting requirements for both types tend to be similar, but may be less onerous for the second type.

Forms of account

In order to illustrate the main differences in the way the ownership interest is presented, and the division of profit shown, in our three kinds of business organization, let us use the figures in Table 3.1.

The figures in Chapter 3 relate to the business of a sole trader. The normal way of showing the ownership interest in the balance sheet would be as in Table 5.1 (though one would usually, in such a presentation, be dealing with the results for a year rather than a week).

Table 5.1 *Balance sheet of sole trader*
Ownership section

Capital	£
Balance at beginning of period	110
Profit for the period as shown in profit and loss account	23
	133
Drawings during the period	10
Balance at end of period	123

Here the profit for the period is merged at the end of the period with the rest of the ownership interest, drawings for the period being deducted from the sum of opening capital and profit. In this case the reconciliation of the closing figure from last period's balance sheet with that for this period is shown in the balance sheet. The rest of the balance sheet would show the assets and liabilities in the usual way. The profit and loss account would be as in Table 3.5.

Let us now consider the same business carried on by a company. We will assume that the share capital subscribed by the shareholders was £80, so that the remaining £30 at the beginning of the period is a reserve – one can assume it represents profits made in the past which have been retained in the business. We will also assume that all the shares have been fully paid up and have each a nominal or par value of £0·25. Finally we will assume that the capital of £80 is the maximum nominal amount which the company is legally authorized to issue for the time being. The profit for the period is, as before, £23, and a *dividend* of £10 has been paid. The ownership section of the balance sheet at the end of the period would appear as in Table 5.2. The general form of the profit and loss account for the period, as it would be seen by the shareholders, would appear as in Table 5.3. (We are ignoring tax and other matters of detail.)

Table 5.2 *Balance sheet of limited company*
Ownership section

	£
Share capital, authorized and issued	
320 ordinary shares of 25p fully paid	80
Reserves*	43
	123

	£
* Balance of profit retained at beginning of period	30
Profit for the period retained, as shown in profit and loss account	13
Balance of profit retained at end of period	43

Table 5.3 *Profit and loss account of limited company*

	£
Profit for the period	23
Dividend on ordinary shares: 3·125p per share	10
Profit retained	13

The equivalent sections of partnership accounts tend to be somewhat more complicated and have some features in common with both sole traders and companies.

Let us use the same figures as before but assume the business is owned, and capital provided, by two partners, *X* and *Y*, who each contributed £40 to the continuing capital of the business. They have agreed to share profits equally, and to make drawings equally. The ownership section of the balance sheet is shown in Table 5.4.

Table 5.4 *Balance sheet of partnership*
Ownership section

	£ X	£ Y	£ Total
Capital accounts	40·00	40·00	80·00
Current accounts			
Balance at beginning of period	15·00	15·00	
Share of profit for the period			
as shown in profit and loss account	11·50	11·50	
	26·50	26·50	
Drawings for the period	5·00	5·00	
Balance at end of the period	21·50	21·50	43·00
			123·00

The part of the profit and loss account showing the appropriation of profit will appear as in Table 5.5.

Table 5.5 *Profit and loss appropriation account of partnership*

		£
Profit for the period		23·00
Partners' shares:		
X one half	11·50	
Y one half	11·50	23·00

Recent developments

The forms of presentation outlined above have dealt with specific parts of the accounting reports that show the ownership interest and the division of profit. The presentation of the remaining parts of the accounts (illustrated in other chapters) does not differ greatly as between different kinds of organization, though that of companies is more standardized. Forms traditional in Britain tend to differ in matters of detail from those in other countries, each of which tends to have its own approach. Such differences do not affect content greatly. However, because the laws of different countries differ, there is necessarily some difference in the content of accounts. There is now growing pressure from various directions towards increased international uniformity in presentation, in content, and in the precise conventions adopted for the valuation of assets and measurement of profit of companies.

Action taken by the European Economic Community (EEC) to harmonize accounting practice will influence and to some extent change British company accounting practice, and in the longer run this will no doubt influence the way in which accounts of other types of organization are prepared. The EEC *Directives* will have the force of law, but so far as British accounting is concerned the changes are likely to be mainly of detail.

A second important influence comes from the establishment of *Statements of Standard Accounting Practice*. These are statements on accounting forms and procedures, developed by committees or boards set up by the professional bodies of accountants acting alone (as in Britain) or jointly with outside interests (as in the United States). The object is to eliminate or reduce arbitrary variations in practice which may mislead or make the interpretation of accounts more difficult. These standards do not have the direct force of law, but accountants who do not follow them may be in trouble with their professional bodies except where there are good reasons (noted in the accounting reports themselves) not to do so. Companies may be required to follow such standards, either under stock exchange rules (if they wish their shares to be listed), as in Britain, or by a legal supervisory body such as the Securities and Exchange Commission (SEC) in the United States.

There is now also an International Accounting Standards body, created by the cooperation of accountants in different countries, whose aim is to introduce greater uniformity internationally.

Views differ as to the usefulness and even desirability of imposing uniformity of procedures where opinion may differ widely, and where it is important not to stifle the development of improved methods through undue rigidity. It would probably be generally accepted, however, that the publication of well-drafted standards at least has the merit of making available to all who use the accounts that follow such standards an explanation and description of the assumptions made and methods used in their preparation.

A major feature of accounting standards is the requirement that a company shall, in its published accounts, state its *accounting policies* – the methods and assumptions it has used in the preparation of the accounts. This statement indicates the particular methods that have been used in applying standard practice and gives explanations of any departures from standard practice.*

* See for example *Statement of Standard Accounting Practice No. 2* issued by the accountancy bodies in Britain and Ireland.

6 Business accounts – 2

Transactions of a manufacturing business

We shall now analyse the transactions of a small manufacturing business carried on by a company. The data will again relate to a week's transactions, from one Saturday to the following Saturday. We shall assume that the business is run by a shareholder–manager.* There are two employees, one of whom is employed in the workshop and one in the office, and both the workshop and office are rented. The employees are paid weekly, on Friday. All money received is paid into the bank and all payments are made by cheque. The only equipment used consists of loose tools. We have:

Opening figures on the first Saturday night

	£
Loose tools	60
Stocks:	
Raw materials	130
Work in progress	80
Finished goods	70
Trade debtors	40
Cash at bank	25
Trade creditors	30
Share capital	300
Retained profit	75

Transactions

Monday   (a) Sold on credit, for £74, finished goods of balance sheet value £50.

Tuesday   (b) Received £30 from trade debtors.

---

* We shall assume for simplicity that the shareholder–manager is at present not being paid any remuneration. Naturally he will have dividend expectations, however.

Wednesday   (c) Paid £25 to trade creditors.

Thursday   (d) Bought raw materials on credit at a cost of £20.

Friday   (e) Recorded the fact that raw materials, of balance sheet value £47, had been used in production, thus reducing the value of raw material stock, with an equivalent increase in the value of work in progress.

                (f) Recorded the fact that some of the tools had been partially worn out in production work. The loss in value estimated at £5 for the week, this being treated as causing an equivalent increase in value of the work in progress.

                (g) Paid weekly wages, £26; half this amount, £13, representing the wage of the operative in the workshop, treated as creating an equivalent increase in the value of work in progress.

                (h) Paid weekly rent, £8; half of this, £4, the rent of the workshop, treated as creating an equivalent increase in the value of work in progress.

                (i) Recorded the fact that during the week part of the work in progress had been completed, the balance sheet value of this being £57.

Saturday   No transactions.

Transactions (a), (b) and (c) are similar to those already discussed, except that the business is selling goods that it has manufactured instead of goods bought for resale. Transaction (d) is new: raw materials have been bought for manufacturing purposes. This transaction affects the balance sheet in the same way as the purchase of goods for resale, and the valuation conventions are similar: that is, the balance sheet value is the original cost of the material. (The same treatment would have been given to the purchase of manufactured components.)

During the week, some of the raw materials are taken from store for production purposes (e). To record this we reduce the value of the asset *raw material* and increase, by the same amount, the asset *work in progress*. 'Work in progress' is the term used to describe partly manufactured products in any state of completion, from unworked raw material that has just been taken out of the store and placed on the production floor, to goods that have been completed but have not been finally transferred to the finished goods store or to the customer. The raw material figure in the balance sheet shows the value of the goods that should be in the raw material store, and the work in progress figure shows the value of the work that should be on the production floor: thus these figures can, among other things, be used as part of a system of control over valuable objects.

The value of work in progress is built up from the value placed on the raw material used for the work in question, together with an amount (calculated on a conventional basis) for the cost of labour services and the services of other factors of production (workshop space and tools) that have contributed to the work up to date.

It is assumed that the wages paid to the workshop operative measure the value added to the product by his work, and the amount of the wages is therefore added to the work in progress valuation (g). If, however, he only worked part of the time (e.g. because business was slack) but was paid for the whole week, only a proportion of his wages, appropriate to the work done, would be added to the value of work-in-progress; the rest would be treated, not as value added, but as an expense or loss in the same way as the wages of the office worker discussed below.

The services of the workshop contribute to the production. The workshop rent for the period is, therefore, also added to the value of the work in progress (h). Here, too, if the available time during the week is not wholly occupied in production, only a proportion will be added, the rest being treated as lost, i.e. as a general expense that does not add to the value of production.

It is assumed that in the course of production some of the manufacturing tools have been physically used up, or have had their future usefulness reduced. The value thus used up is similarly added to the balance sheet value of work in progress (f). The tools themselves will usually be valued at their original cost, and the loss in value (or *depreciation*) will be calculated as a proportion of this original cost. The value added to the work in progress in this respect is therefore part of the original cost of the tools. Here again only part of the total depreciation for the period may be added to the value of the work in progress if the tools have not been in normal use all the week but are assumed nevertheless to have lost value through deterioration or obsolescence.

During the week, the manufacture of a certain physical quantity of work in progress is completed and the balance sheet value of this, calculated by summing the components just described, is transferred to the classification *finished goods* (i). This implies that each time additional value is allotted to the work in progress it is allocated to a specific product or set of products: the £13 of wages cost added to work in progress for the week will, for example, be divided among the various jobs done on the basis of the time the workman has spent on each; the raw material cost will be allotted to the particular products for which the material is used; the depreciation of tools and the rent will be allocated in some convenient way that is thought to provide a reasonable indication of their contribution to output – for example, on the basis of the time spent on each unit of output in the workshop, so that a job that has taken half the available working time in the week may have half the workshop rent added to its cost.*

The value of the finished goods calculated in this way is sometimes called the *manufacturing cost of production*, or *works cost of production*. These terms are used to indicate that the balance sheet value has been calculated without taking into consideration the *administrative overhead costs* – expenses such as office wages and rent that are less closely concerned with the physical production activities than are the workshop expenses. Needless to say, the cost of production so calculated will only by accident be equal to the saleable value of the goods and in the general case will be less.

That part of the value assigned to the finished goods which consists of the material used in the product and the wages of the operatives directly concerned with making it is called the *prime cost, direct cost* or (somewhat misleadingly) *marginal cost*.†

When the finished goods are sold the balance sheet values are adjusted in the same way as when part of a stock of goods originally bought for resale is sold (*a*). Like goods bought for resale, the manufactured goods are, as we have just seen, normally valued on the basis of original cost, though the calculation of this cost is more complicated than in the case of goods which are merely bought for resale without processing, and involves a greater number of arbitrary assumptions. In general the manufacturer will so plan that the average of this original cost, taken over the whole output, is below the sales value of the goods by a *gross profit margin* sufficient to meet the remaining expenses (here the office wages and rent), to remunerate

* The purpose of such allocations (and their usefulness and significance) raise important economic questions that must be studied when the economic and management aspects of accounting are considered. Here we are concerned with the procedures.

† Prime or direct cost may also include the cost of other services than labour – e.g. power – where these are incurred for, and only for, a specific unit of product.

the management, and to give an economic return on the capital value invested in the business.*

It is a matter of convention how much of the expenditure recorded in the accounts of a business in a given period is treated as a change in asset structure (as where a fall in cash is balanced by a rise in, say, work in progress) and how much is treated as an expense (as where a fall in cash is balanced by a fall in the ownership interest). As sales are made, so that the cash or debtors rise and the stock of finished goods falls, the balance sheet assets *less* liabilities – the net assets – rise by the excess of the sales value over the finished goods balance sheet valuation. In so far as amounts spent on rent, wages, etc., have already been treated as an expense and *written off*, that is removed from the balance sheet by a reduction in the ownership interest, the profit reported when the sale is finally recorded will be so much the greater, since the book value of the stock sold will be correspondingly lower.

Different valuation methods may thus alter the distribution of profit reported as between different accounting periods. This is because a higher stock valuation in period 1 (i.e. the allocation of more, rather than less, expense to the work in progress value) will raise the amount of the ownership interest at the end of period 1, but will reduce it by the same amount in the period in which the stock is sold, e.g. in period 2. The longer the interval of time considered, however, the less relatively will a change in the method of valuation of work in progress and finished goods at the beginning and end of the period affect the aggregate net profit reported during the interval, since these stock valuations will be an increasingly smaller proportion of the sales revenue as the period lengthens.†

---

* In the language of economic theory, management remuneration and a return on capital sufficient to make it worth while to continue the business are both 'costs'. Here accounting and economic *language* (though not necessarily *ideas*) differ, for an accountant would not usually call any part of what he classifies as net profit, a 'cost'. (In our example we have assumed for simplicity that any management remuneration has to be met out of profit. In the case of companies, however, the management usually receive salaries, even when the same people are both shareholders and managers: such salaries are 'costs' to the accountant because the company is a distinct legal entity.)

† This discussion of stock valuation methods must be regarded as provisional. A number of important qualifications and amplifications, some of which we shall examine later, and some of which must be left for further reading, have necessarily been omitted at this stage. For example, the work in progress value is sometimes determined by summing only the raw materials and the wages of

Double entry analysis

We shall now summarize in double entry form the opening figures and the week's transactions given at the beginning of this chapter, using the kind of analysis that was employed in Table 3.1. This analysis is shown in Table 6.1. The reader should check the entries in this table against the original information.

Accounts (1), (2), (3), (4) and (5) in Table 6.1 relate to assets. Accounts (7), (8) and (9) relate to claims, (7) to claims of creditors, and (8) and (9) to the ownership interest. The account in column (6), which shows transactions with the bank, is peculiar, in that for part of the period it records an asset and for part a liability. It will be noticed that when all the bank transactions are taken together there is a net excess of value on the credit side: cash payments are greater than the sum of the opening balance and receipts. This means that the business owes money to the bank at the end of the week: the bank has then a claim on the business. Thus the double entry rules allow an account which records an asset at one time to record a claim at another.

The balance sheets which would be obtained if the balances were extracted from Table 6.1 each day are shown in Table 6.2. The first row of figures of Table 6.1 gives us the data for the opening balance sheet, shown in the first column of Table 6.2. The final row of figures of Table 6.1. gives us the final column of Table 6.2. Each intervening column in Table 6.2 can be obtained in the same way by summing the columns of Table 6.1 down to the appropriate line and taking the difference between the total debits and total credits for each account.

operatives directly concerned with production, all other expenses being treated 'as if' they were lost, and written off: stocks are valued 'at direct cost'. This obviously gives a lower value for work in progress and a correspondingly lower initial figure for profit than the method used in our example; but this is compensated for when the finished goods are sold, for the profit then shown is correspondingly larger. Again, there are strong arguments for abandoning the original cost basis of valuation in favour of one based on current market prices. This is discussed in Chapter 12. Our main concern here is to understand the kind of procedures that are used in the construction of accounting reports. These procedures can be adapted to any method of valuation selected. The valuation methods we have described so far conform with standard practice under the historical cost accounting convention. Evidently they must be known by anyone who wishes to understand accounting reports; but they are not necessarily the best, and the fact that they are described here does not imply that they are approved by the author as appropriate in all circumstances.

Table 6.1 Double entry analysis

	(1) Loose tools		(2) Raw materials		(3) Work in progress		(4) Finished goods		(5) Trade debtors		(6) Cash at bank		(7) Trade creditors		(8) Share capital		(9) Profit and loss	
	£	£	£	£	£	£	£	£	£	£	£	£	£	£	£	£	£	£
Opening balances	60		130		80		70		40		25			30		300		75
Monday (a)									74									
Tuesday (b)								50			30		25					24
Wednesday (c)										30		25						
Thursday (d)			20											20				
Friday (e)				47	47		57											
(f)		5			5													
(g)					13							26					13	
(h)					4							8					4	
(i)						57												
Totals	60	5	150	47	149	57	127	50	114	30	55	59	25	50	—	300	17	99
Closing balances	55		103		92		77		84		4		25		300		82	

Table 6.2 *Balance sheets at the close of business*

	£ Sat	Mon	Tues	Wed	Thurs	Fri	Sat
Loose tools	60	60	60	60	60	55	55
Raw materials	130	130	130	130	150	103	103
Work in progress	80	80	80	80	80	92	92
Finished goods	70	20	20	20	20	77	77
Trade debtors	40	114	84	84	84	84	84
Bank	25	25	55	30	30	–	–
Total assets	405	429	429	404	424	411	411
Trade creditors	30	30	30	5	25	25	25
Bank	–	–	–	–	–	4	4
Total liabilities	30	30	30	5	25	29	29
Share capital	300	300	300	300	300	300	300
Profit and loss	75	99	99	99	99	82	82
Total ownership interest	375	399	399	399	399	382	382
Total claims or finance	405	429	429	404	424	411	411

The double entry analysis of Table 6.1 can also be used to derive the daily and weekly flow of funds. This is shown in Table 6.3. The figures in this can be checked from rows (*a*) to (*i*) in Table 6.1 (Remember that the + and − signs in the lower section of the funds statements all relate to rises and falls in claims, themselves negative in our double entry scheme, and are therefore of the opposite sign to that which we should give to the corresponding figures in the double entry accounts of Table 6.1.) The balance sheet for each day, as shown in Table 6.2, could, of course, have been built up from the balance sheet of the preceding day by applying the differences in Table 6.3.

These illustrations are not intended to show in detail how the figures in balance sheets are built up in practice from the records of a business: they are intended to bring out the relationships between the various kinds of accounting statement and to show in principle how transactions can be conveniently summarized and classified. Nevertheless the procedure just described does correspond with the

Table 6.3 *Funds statements*

	£						
	Sat–Mon	Mon–Tues	Tues–Wed	Wed–Thurs	Thurs–Fri	Fri–Sat	Week
Loose tools	–	–	–	–	– 5	–	– 5
Raw materials	–	–	–	+ 20	– 47	–	– 27
Work in progress	–	–	–	–	+ 12	–	+ 12
Finished goods	– 50	–	–	–	+ 57	–	+ 7
Trade debtors	+ 74	– 30	–	–	–	–	+ 44
Bank	–	+ 30	– 25	–	– 34	–	– 29*
Change in assets	+ 24	–	– 25	+ 20	– 17	–	+ 2
Trade creditors	–	–	– 25	+ 20	–	–	– 5
Capital	–	–	–	–	–	–	–
Profit	+ 24	–	–	–	– 17	–	+ 7
Change in claims	+ 24	–	– 25	+ 20	– 17	–	+ 2

* This net change over the week converts an asset of £25 on the first Saturday into a liability of £4 on the second Saturday: see Table 6.2.

normal accounting process in the sense that the accounting system must provide for the collection of the raw data (exemplified by the information given at the beginning of the chapter), for its assembly and analysis (exemplified by the classified summary in Table 6.1), and for its presentation in the accounting reports for the use of the management and others, of the type shown in Tables 6.2 and 6.3.

We can now proceed further by extracting profit and loss reports from the data in Column (9) of Table 6.1. The result is summarized, day by day, and for the whole week, in the first five rows of figures of Table 6.4: here we have the revenue and expenses which are the components of the net profit earned. In the remaining rows of the table – the appropriation section – the retained profit at the beginning of each day is added, giving the retained profit at the end of each day, while the last column gives similar information for the week as a whole. A line is provided for dividends paid to the shareholder: in this example they happen to be zero, but if they existed they would reduce the retained profit.

The funds statement for the week, drawn up for presentation as a report, is shown in Table 6.5. In this statement, the depreciation of

Table 6.4 *Profit and loss statements*

	£						
	Sat–Mon	Mon–Tues	Tues–Wed	Wed–Thurs	Thurs–Fri	Fri–Sat	Week
Revenue							
Gross profit	24	–	–	–	–	–	24
Expenses							
Rent	–	–	–	–	4	–	4
Wages	–	–	–	–	13	–	13
	–	–	–	–	17	–	17
Profit for period	24	–	–	–	−17	–	7
Retained profit at beginning of period	75	99	99	99	99	82	75
	99	99	99	99	82	82	82
Dividends	–	–	–	–	–	–	–
Retained profit at end of period	99	99	99	99	82	82	82

Table 6.5 *Funds statement, week ending ——*

Sources of funds	£
Profit for week, retained in business	7
Depreciation of loose tools	5
Decrease in raw materials	27
	39

Uses of funds	
Increase in work in progress	12
Increase in finished goods	7
Increase in debtors	44
Decrease in creditors	5
	68
Decrease in cash	29

C

loose tools appears as a source of funds. This is because depreciation is not a cash outlay, nor does it result in a change in any other asset or liability than tools. It has already been deducted from the revenue in arriving at the retained profit. It is 'added back' because it is the profit before deducting depreciation which accounts for the net change in cash, stocks, debtors and creditors in the period. (This point is dealt with further in Chapter 7.)

Revenue and expense accounts

The profit statements of Table 6.4 were obtained from the ledger account for profit and loss, Column (9) of Table 6.1. It was easy to analyse the items in this column into their appropriate classes because there were only a few transactions. In practice there are many transactions, so it is convenient to split up the profit and loss account and maintain a separate ledger account for each class of transaction for which a separate total is likely to be useful. The ledger accounts, it must be remembered, constitute the controlling records that are built up from the various sources of original data, and from which accounting reports will be extracted as they are required.

Thus, instead of the single ledger account in Column (9) of Table 6.1, we could have three separate accounts for gross profit, wages, and rent, respectively, together with an additional account to show the effect of combining the three – that is, to summarize the information needed for presentation in the top part of Table 6.4 (down to the 'profit for period'). A fifth account – the *appropriation account* – could summarize the information for the remaining part of the table.

Table 6.6 shows how these ledger accounts would appear. The figures that appear in the various columns of that table all appeared in the profit column of Table 6.1, but each is now shown under its own classified heading (see items (*a*), (*g*) and (*h*) in Table 6.6). (We must imagine that Column (9) of Table 6.1 has disappeared and been replaced by Columns (10) to (14) of Table 6.6.)

At the end of the period each column is totalled and the balance is entered. These balances are then transferred to the profit and loss column (see items (*j*), (*k*) and (*l*)). This transfer (which can be regarded as a reclassification of part of the ownership interest) is made by cancelling the balance under the original classification – e.g. rent – by inserting an entry equal, but of opposite sign, to the

Table 6.6 *Extension of double entry summary*

(replacing Column (9) of Table 6.1)

	(10) Gross profit		(11) Office wages		(12) Office rent		(13) Profit and loss		(14) Appro-priation	
	£	£	£	£	£	£	£	£	£	£
Opening balance	–	–	–	–	–	–	–	–	–	75
(a) Gross profit		24								
(g) Wages			13							
(h) Rent					4					
	–	24	13	–	4	–	–	–	–	75
Balances	–	24	13	–	4	–	–	–	–	75
(j) Transfer	24							24		
(k) ,,			13				13			
(l) ,,						4	4			
	24	24	13	13	4	4	17	24	–	75
Balances	–	–	–	–	–	–	–	7	–	75
(m) Transfer							7			7
							7	7	–	82
Closing balance	–	–	–	–	–	–	–	–	–	82

The above analysis shows how the various components of the profit section of the ownership claim can, when they are first recorded, be allotted to separate accounts in order to facilitate the analysis of the sources of profit and loss. They can then be reclassified to produce the profit and loss account. Finally the net profit for the period can be reclassified with the undistributed profit at the beginning of the period in the appropriation account.

existing balance, and making an entry of the same amount and sign as the existing balance in the new ledger account – e.g. profit and loss. Thus the rent debit balance of £4 is cancelled by a credit item of £4, and a new debit of £4 is entered in the profit and loss account.* When these entries have been made a balance is struck on the profit and loss account, giving the profit earned for the period, here £7.

The appropriation account in Column (14) shows as an opening balance the ownership claim for retained profit at the beginning of

---

* Remember that this rent is being treated as, in effect, a reduction in the ownership claim: the money has been spent – the owner can no longer claim it. This is shown as a debit – an offset against the ownership interest credit.

the period; the profit figure for the period is transferred to this account from the profit and loss account (item (*m*)); the closing balance is the sum of the two figures. The profit and loss and appropriation accounts thus correspond with the report in Table 6.4. They show the form of the book-keeping records which provide the information for this report.

The analysis in Table 6.6 may seem to the reader repetitive, adding little or nothing to the information we already have. This is because we are dealing with a very simple example, and in particular with one in which each class of transaction is represented by one figure only. This is very far from being the case in real life. One must imagine the single items here shown in each of the columns headed 'gross profit', 'office wages', and 'office rent' replaced by a large number of figures, and the three columns themselves multiplied perhaps 100 or 1,000 times. The need for a detailed system of classification is then more apparent.

Cost of sales

In practice it is also convenient to subdivide the ledger account that we have called 'gross profit'. The gross profit on a transaction is the resultant of two components, one debit – the cost of the goods sold (equal to the amount credited to the finished goods account), and one credit – the sales value (equal to the amount debited to the debtor or received in cash); the double entry for each such transaction was completed in the above example by crediting the gross profit as one item to a 'gross profit' account. In practice we use two accounts, one called 'cost of goods sold' or 'cost of sales' and one called 'sales', in which the respective debits and credits are collected. This is helpful if one wishes to analyse and study the sales figures by themselves, and to examine the relationship of the sales revenue to the cost of sales. It is normal to show these two components separately in profit and loss reports to management. Their separation is also convenient from a book-keeping or data-processing point of view, in that the original data for the two components are in practice usually collected through quite different channels: the sales value information is derived from the section of the enterprise responsible for invoicing, and the cost of sales from the accounting section responsible for costing information.

Hence, we may replace the gross profit account in Table 6.6 by the two accounts shown in Table 6.7, the separate balances of which

Table 6.7 *Alternative treatment of sales and cost of sales*

(dividing into two accounts Column (10) and amending
Column (13) of Table 6.6)

	(10a) Cost of sales		(10b) Sales		(13) Profit and loss	
	£	£	£	£	£	£
(a) Cost of sales/Sales	50			74		
(n) Transfer		50			50	
(p) ,,			74			74

are both transferred to the profit and loss account at the end of the accounting period.

The expanded report for presentation to management would run on these lines:

	£	£
Sales		74
less Cost of sales		50
Gross profit		24
less General expenses:		
Office rent	4	
Office wages	13	17
Profit		7

The first three lines of this statement form what it has been customary to call the *trading account*.

T accounts

We shall now show how the above transactions would appear when entered in T accounts. The set of T accounts is given in Table 6.8. Readers are recommended to check the items from the former tables into the accounts in Table 6.8, ticking off each figure in the old and in the new accounts as it is checked.

In Table 6.8 we have provided each item with a reference letter, as before; we have also inserted against each item the name of the account in which its contra (the opposite side of the double entry) appears. Thus item (d), £20, on the debit side of raw materials

Table 6.8

Loose tools

	£		£
Balance b/d	60	(f) Work in progress	5
		Balance c/d	55
	60		60
Balance b/d	55		

Raw materials

	£		£
Balance b/d	130	(e) Work in progress	47
(d) Creditors	20	Balance c/d	103
	150		150
Balance b/d	103		

Work in progress

	£		£
Balance b/d	80	(i) Finished goods	57
(e) Raw materials	47	Balance c/d	92
(f) Tools	5		
(g) Bank	13		
(h) Bank	4		
	149		149
Balance b/d	92		

Finished goods

	£		£
Balance b/d	70	(a) Cost of Sales	50
(i) Work in progress	57	Balance c/d	77
	127		127
Balance b/d	77		

Trade debtors

	£		£
Balance b/d	40	(b) Bank	30
(a) Sales	74	Balance c/d	84
	114		114
Balance b/d	84		

Cash at bank

	£		£
Balance b/d	25	(c) Creditors	25
(b) Debtors	30	(g) Work in progress	13
Balance c/d	4	(g) Office wages	13
		(h) Work in progress	4
		(h) Office rent	4
	59		59
		Balance b/d	4

Trade creditors

	£		£
(c) Bank	25	Balance b/d	30
Balance c/d	25	(d) Raw materials	20
	50		50
		Balance b/d	25

Share capital

	£		£
		Balance b/d	300

Cost of sales				Sales			
	£		£		£		£
(a) Finished goods	50	(n) Profit and loss	50	(p) Profit and loss	74	(a) Debtors	74

Office wages				Office rent			
	£		£		£		£
(g) Bank	13	(k) Profit and loss	13	(h) Bank	4	(l) Profit and loss	4

Profit and loss				Appropriation			
	£		£		£		£
(n) Cost of sales	50	(p) Sales	74	Balance c/d	82	Balance b/d	75
(k) Office wages	13					(m) Profit and loss	7
(l) Office rent	4				82		82
(m) Appropriation	7					Balance b/d	82
	74		74				

account, is also referenced 'creditors', showing that the equivalent credit is in the trade creditors account; the latter is similarly referenced 'raw materials'. This is the traditional method of referencing in double entry book-keeping. In a good deal of practical book-keeping the only reference needed against an item in a double entry account is a code number or letter, and, if the date of the transaction is not implied by the reference number, a date, so that it is possible to trace each entry back to the original information from which it was derived. It is often useful, however, e.g. when analysing data in working papers for the preparation of accounting reports, to use the traditional method of referencing each debit or credit to its corresponding credit or debit as we have done here.

The trial balance

On completion of a set of accounting entries it is often convenient, as a check on arithmetical accuracy, to make sure the sums of the debit and the credit balances agree, by listing each in a *trial balance* and comparing the totals. The trial balance for the above set of T accounts, proving the arithmetical accuracy of the work (subject to the existence of any compensating errors – errors of equal magnitude but opposite sign), is as follows:

	£	£
Loose tools	55	
Raw materials	103	
Work in progress	92	
Finished goods	77	
Trade debtors	84	
Cash at bank		4
Trade creditors		25
Capital		300
Appropriation		82
	411	411

Notice that in the trial balance, debit balances appear on the debit (left-hand) side and credit balances on the credit (right-hand) side as in the T ledger accounts. In this respect the trial balance differs from a formal balance sheet, which may be presented in any convenient way, but in Britain (for historical reasons) often has debits on the right-hand side and credits on the left-hand side.

Time-lags in accounting records

Balance sheet changes reflect both internal revaluations and re-arrangements of resources (such as a transfer from the raw material to the work in progress classification) and external transactions (such as the sale of goods to customers or purchases from suppliers). Both types of balance sheet change are usually recorded in the ledger accounts only at the end of given intervals. It is not normally prac-ticable to keep all the accounting records adjusted continuously as economic circumstances change (though electronic computers are bringing us closer to being able to achieve this, where the cost is justified). For example, in a manufacturing business, raw materials may move into production throughout the week, but the fact may be entered in the formal accounting records as if the whole change occurred at the end of the working week (here Friday).* Similarly,

---

* Though, of course, continuous subsidiary records will have to be maintained so that the information can be collected and summarized.

the wages accruing to the labour force for work done throughout the week, and the corresponding increase imputed to the work in progress value, may not be recorded until the wages are paid at the end of the week.*

---

* But if payment is made after the end of an accounting period – i.e. a period for which an accounting report is made – it is necessary to recognize in the balance sheet the amounts owing at that date: the dates of the accounting reports may therefore determine when such transactions are recorded. This is discussed in Chapter 9.

7 Current assets and liabilities

All the assets so far discussed have (with one exception – loose tools) been what are called *current assets*. The main kinds of current assets are: stocks of all kinds (sometimes called *inventories*); trade debtors; cash; investments held temporarily as an interest-yielding substitute for cash; and payments in advance (or prepayments) – services to be received after balance sheet date which have already been paid for, such as insurance cover extending beyond that date.

Current assets are thought of as assets that are already in cash or near-cash form, or within a short period will be converted, directly or indirectly, into cash, or will otherwise yield their services to the business shortly. A 'short period' here means generally less than a year. There are, however, exceptions, as when it is normal to hold stock for a longer period than a year before sale.

The fundamental reason for distinguishing current assets from *fixed assets* (discussed in Chapter 8) is linked to the question of liquidity. Changes in the value of current assets are likely to have a swift repercussion on the capacity of the business to pay its creditors as they fall due, to meet unexpected expenses, or to take advantage of unexpected opportunities. A sudden drop in the saleable value of stock may quickly create a serious cash crisis and undermine the planned schedule of activities.

The separate classification of current assets, and the study of changes in them from period to period – as in a funds statement – is an important part of the interpretation of accounts and of financial control.

It is no doubt for this reason that company law requires such assets to be distinguished in statutory accounts.

It follows from the definition that the assets classified as current in a particular case will depend on the nature of the business. Motor lorries in the course of construction or awaiting sale in an automobile manufacturing factory are current assets – in this case stocks of work in progress or finished goods. The same lorries when owned by a transport company are not current assets.

Balance sheet values of current assets

It has already been indicated that under the historical cost system of accounting, stocks are normally valued on the basis of their original cost, though the precise manner of calculation of cost may vary to some extent. This must now be qualified. If the market value of stock has fallen to a point such that it appears that the ultimate selling value, after making a deduction for expenses of sale, is below the cost, the balance sheet value is reduced to the net realizable value. For this reason the standard historical cost valuation convention for stocks is known as the *cost or lower market value* rule. There is thus an asymmetry: rises in market value that occur before sale are ignored, but falls, if greater than a certain amount, are taken into consideration. This asymmetry is due to a traditional bias towards conservatism or 'prudence' in accounting practice.

Sometimes the estimated current market replacement cost is taken as the maximum permissible balance sheet value, instead of the estimated net realizable value. This is not, however, a standard practice under historical cost accounting in Britain.

The cost or lower market value rule can be applied to a particular class of stock as a whole or to individual units. Suppose that the stock consisted of three items and that the data relating to these were:

	Cost	Market value
	£	£
X	10	7
Y	8	9
Z	14	11
	32	27

If the cost or lower market value rule were applied to the stock as a whole, the balance sheet valuation would be £27, this being below £32. In this case the increase in value of *Y* would partly offset the fall in value of *X* and *Z*. If, however, each item were considered separately we should have:

	Cost or lower market value
	£
X	7
Y	8
Z	11
	26

This gives a lower, and more conservative, valuation and is now considered standard practice. Where it is not practicable to value items on a one-by-one basis, the method is applied to groups of similar assets.

Where it becomes necessary to reduce the value of stock below its existing book value, there is an equivalent reduction in the profit. It would be reasonable to open a special account to which such losses could be debited, the balance on which at the end of the year would be transferred to the cost of sales account. If the total of such losses were shown in the profit and loss report as a separate part of the cost of sales, this would indicate the extent to which the business had incurred losses through failure to anticipate price changes or (where the fall in value was due to deterioration or obsolescence of stocks, or errors in manufacture) through other kinds of failure. Often, however, such losses are merged in the cost of sales figure.

Whatever valuation convention is used in a given case, accountants lay great stress on the preservation of consistency in method from year to year. For although results will differ with the use of different conventions, and will therefore require different interpretations, changes in methods will introduce additional, arbitrary, effects. Sometimes there are reasons for changing the particular conventions employed; in such cases it is standard accounting practice to include in any profit and loss report a statement of the effect of the change on the figures. Thus, a change from an 'all in' to an 'item by item' interpretation of the cost or lower market value made at the end of a given year might well reduce the profit reported for the year. The profit and loss report should contain a statement drawing attention to the amount of the reduction so caused. This rule of consistency is not limited to stock valuation: it applies to the whole of accounting.

The historical cost valuation conventions applied to stock are, with qualifications, applied to other current assets. The general rule followed is that the value to be used is the value at the time the asset is acquired, less any amount needed to reduce that figure to its current realizable value. Thus, debts are included at the face value when the debt was created (e.g. by sale of goods), less an allowance for any expected loss in collection.*

The services arising from prepayments are valued by apportioning the total cost over time on a straight-line basis and treating the proportion relating to the period after the balance sheet date as the value of the asset at that date.

Classification of liabilities

Like assets, liabilities are classified as current and non-current (or deferred). Current liabilities – the only type so far included in our examples – are usually defined as those expected to be settled within one year of the balance sheet date. Most creditors for goods and services supplied fall into this class. For consistency, amounts which are to be repaid within a year should be so classified, even if their original term was longer, so that a loan originally for ten years should be classified as current when the last year of its life is reached.

It is considered good practice – and may be required by law – to sub-classify the longer-term, non-current liabilities according to their terms, so that we find amounts payable between one and five years away are shown by companies separately from longer-term ones.

Certain liabilities are likely to be classified separately because of their special nature. For example, bank overdrafts, the repayment dates of which are often uncertain, are shown separately.

Among liabilities are found *provisions* – figures which represent liabilities that are known to exist but the amounts of which cannot be determined with substantial accuracy (such as a provision for taxation not yet assessed or for a possible liability arising from an uncompleted lawsuit). Such provisions for liabilities must be distinguished from *provisions for depreciation*, which are the amounts by which fixed asset values have been reduced (see Chapter 8).

---

* It should be emphasized again that here we are only describing, in outline, the normal historical cost conventions. Many variants are found in practice, and alternative conventions have been advocated and in some cases introduced. In particular, the choice of method will now be affected by the existence of statements of standard accounting practice.

8   Fixed assets and depreciation

Fixed assets

We now consider an example where the main asset is a *fixed asset*; and instead of all the longer-term finance being supplied by the owner, some is provided by an outside lender so that we have a non-current liability. There are no other liabilities and the only current asset is cash.

A fixed asset is one that is acquired with the intention of holding it for use in the business, usually for a longer period than a year, and often much longer. It is not held with the intention of trading in it, like stock, or for the purpose of embodiment in manufactured stock, like a raw material or a component.

Let us assume that *A* starts an owner–driver taxi business. His basic asset is a taxi. This is a fixed asset: he does not intend to buy and sell taxis as a normal trading activity. He intends to use it as part of his business equipment.

A buys the taxi partly out of money from his own pocket and partly by borrowing from *B*. His only expenses are for fuel, oil, maintenance, garage, and licences. (As before, we shall use unrealistically small figures to save space.) The summarized financial data for his first year are shown opposite.

No amounts are owing from or to the business at the end of the year except for the loan from *B*. All payments are by cheque, but we shall follow accountants' practice by calling cash at bank simply 'cash'. We shall here, as throughout this book, ignore income tax and other tax.

For convenience we have in this example, unlike the previous ones, condensed the whole of each class of transactions for the period into a single figure. Our data are therefore not chronological from (*a*) to (*f*).

First we carry out the double entry analysis in T account form. The ledger accounts recording and classifying the above information

Opening figures on the morning of 1 January

	£
Cash at bank	1,000
Long-term loan from *B*	400
Capital supplied by *A*	600

Transactions (summarized for the year)

		£
1 Jan	(*a*) Bought a taxi	950
1 Jan to 31 Dec	(*b*) Received and paid into bank fares and tips	1,300
	(*c*) Paid for licences, fuel, oil, repairs, and garage	603
	(*d*) Paid 10% per annum interest on the loan	40
	(*e*) Drew from the business bank account for personal expenses	500

(*f*) *A* intends to sell the taxi and buy a new one at the end of 5 years. He expects the sale price to be £350. He therefore sets the average annual cost of using the taxi, i.e. its average annual fall in value or depreciation, at:

$$\frac{£(950-350)}{5} = \qquad 120*$$

are shown in Table 8.1. The entries include the opening receipts of cash from *A* and *B*, and the corresponding credits to capital and loan accounts. They also include the closing of the revenue and expense accounts, that is the transfer of the various revenue and expense balances to the profit and loss account, and the transfer in turn of the balance of net profit to the credit of capital account and similarly the transfer of drawings to the debit of capital account.

The opening and closing balance sheets are given in Table 8.2. The reader should check that the figures in these correspond respectively to the opening and closing balances in the ledger accounts of Table 8.1.

---

* Compare this figure with the loss in value of the tools in the example at the beginning of Chapter 6.

Table 8.1

Capital					Loan (B)		
	£		£		£		£
(*l*) Drawings	500	Cash	600			Cash	400
Balance c/d	637	(*k*) Profit					
		and loss	537				
	1,137		1,137				
		Balance b/d	637				

Cash at bank					Taxi		
	£		£		£		£
Capital	600	(*a*) Taxi	950	(*a*) Cash	950	(*f*) Depre-	
Loan	400	(*c*) Running				ciation	120
(*b*) Fares	1,300	expenses	603			Balance c/d	830
		(*d*) Interest	40		950		950
		(*e*) Drawings	500	Balance b/d	830		
		Balance c/d	207				
	2,300		2,300				
Balance b/d	207						

Revenue from fares					Running expenses		
	£		£		£		£
(*g*) Profit		(*b*) Cash	1,300	(*c*) Cash	603	(*h*) Profit	
and loss	1,300					and loss	603

Loan interest					Depreciation		
	£		£		£		£
(*d*) Cash	40	(*i*) Profit		(*f*) Taxi	120	(*j*) Profit	
		and loss	40			and loss	120

Profit and loss					Drawings account		
	£		£		£		£
(*h*) Running		(*g*) Fares	1,300	(*e*) Cash	500	(*l*) Capital	500
expenses	603						
(*i*) Loan							
interest	40						
(*j*) Depre-							
ciation	120						
(*k*) Capital	537						
	1,300		1,300				

Table 8.2 *Balance sheets*

| | 1 January | 31 December |
	£	£
Taxi	–	830
Cash at bank	1,000	207
	1,000	1,037
Loan from *B*	400	400
Capital	600	637
	1,000	1,037

The profit and loss report for the owner can be extracted from the double entry profit and loss account. We have:

	£	£
Revenue from fares		1,300
Running expenses	603	
Interest	40	
Depreciation	120	763
Profit for year		537

The difference between this net profit and the drawings is the net profit retained (or 'carried forward') in the business and transferred to capital account.

In the conventional accounting report of a sole trader's business the net profit and the drawings will usually, as noted earlier, be merged in the figure of capital, so that no distinction is made in the closing balance sheet between the original paid-in capital and the retained profit. We have:

	£
Capital, 1 January	600
Net profit for year as shown in profit and loss statement	537
	1,137
Drawings	500
Capital, 31 December	637

A simplified funds statement for the year (excluding the opening items) is as follows:

	£
Taxi	+830
Cash at bank	−793
	+ 37
Profit *less* drawings	+ 37

The rise in value under the heading 'taxi' is the net result of two items, an initial cash expenditure of £950 and an estimated subsequent loss in value (depreciation) of £120.

A more significant way of presenting the funds statement would be as follows:

	£
Cash flow from operations	
Amount representing recovery of depreciation	120
Amount representing net profit	537
	657
Reduction in initial cash balance	793
	1,450
Expenditure on new taxi	950
Drawings	500
	1,450

This brings out clearly that the cash inflow from operations was greater than the net profit by the amount estimated for the depreciation of the taxi during the year.

Depreciation

We shall now consider the financial significance of the depreciation figure. In the above example, the profit retained at the end of the year is £37. The cash balance at that date is £207. Suppose that the remaining £37 of the year's profit is withdrawn on 31 December: we are still left with £170 of cash at the bank.

The balance sheet now reads:

		£
	Taxi	830
	Cash	170
		1,000
	Loan	400
	Capital	600
		1,000

The original cash brought into the business was £1,000. Of this, £950 was spent on the taxi, leaving £50. This £50 has now grown to £170. The increase of £120 in cash is equal in amount to that part of the year's expenses (as shown in the profit and loss report above) not spent in cash, that is, to the depreciation: this is the estimated amount of the fall in value of a fixed asset, the taxi. This is not a current *cash* expense; but we have, so to speak, 'spent' £120 of the taxi's value.

Let us continue the story for the next four years, on the assumption that each year is a replica of the first and that the proprietor withdraws from the business all his net profits as now shown in the accounts. We assume as before that there are no changes in price levels. At the end of the fifth year the balance sheet is as follows:

	£
Taxi	350

This has been reduced (written down) by £120 each year for 5 years $[950-(5 \times 120)=350]$

Cash	650

This has grown by £120 each year $[1,000-950+(5 \times 120)=650]$

	1,000
Loan (unchanged)	400
Capital (unchanged, all reported profit having been withdrawn)	600
	1,000

On the morning of the next day, 1 January of the sixth year, the old taxi is sold for the expected £350. We have then:

	£
Taxi (350 − 350)	–
Cash (650 + 350)	1,000
	1,000
Loan	400
Capital	600
	1,000

We have thus reached the same position as that at which we started, five years ago, and the cycle can begin again.

This demonstrates the nature of the depreciation calculation and its relation to profit determination. It shows that the reported annual level of profit will depend, among other things, upon the convention of depreciation measurement adopted and the assumptions made about the life and ultimate value of the asset.*

Suppose that depreciation of the taxi had been ignored when the profit was calculated. The profit each year would then be reported as £657 (£537 + £120). Suppose this amount was withdrawn from the business each year. At the end of the five years there would not be assets of sufficient value to buy a new taxi, or invest the original amount of finance in some other venture, or repay the loan and withdraw all the original capital. The balance sheet would tell exactly the same story at the end of the first and of each following year, namely:

	£
Taxi	950
Cash	50
	1,000
Loan	400
Capital	600
	1,000

When the taxi was sold at the end of the fifth year, £350 of its balance sheet value would be converted into cash, leaving £600 of apparent value in the balance sheet thus:

* The total depreciation in the five years is £600. This was spread on a straight-line or linear basis, i.e. at a steady rate of £120 per annum. This is the usual convention. Other ways of spreading this £600 over the period may be used; for these reference should be made to texts in the reading list.

	£
Taxi (950 − 350)	600
Cash	400
	1,000
Loan	400
Capital	600
	1,000

But the taxi would have gone and it is clear that the £600 would not correspond, even roughly, to reality. We should have to record a 'book loss' of £600. ('Book' because the real economic loss was incurred earlier: the taxi loses value throughout its life and we are only recognizing belatedly an economic event that has already happened.) The ownership claim is consequently not worth £600 or anything in the neighbourhood of that sum. It is indeed zero. We have, when the balance sheet is adjusted, to show this fact:

		£
Taxi (600 − 600)		–
Cash		400
		400
Loan		400
Capital	600	
Loss	600	–
		400

As it happens, the figures we have chosen are such that in this case there would have been just enough cash left to repay the loan; but this is accidental. In other words, by failing to record the steady fall in value of an asset, *A* could have deceived himself (or others, such as *B*, whose loan is in jeopardy) as to his economic situation.

In a sole trader's business (or partnership business, if the partners so agree) there is, in fact, nothing to prevent an owner from withdrawing from the business a greater sum than the net profit earned, although if he does so he may have to pay money into the business again later if he wishes to carry on, or meet his obligations. The withdrawal of cash may indeed sometimes represent the best use which an owner can make of the surplus cash which has built up, e.g. before the time comes for the replacement of the fixed assets. For the time being he may be able to earn more by using the money outside the business than within; or he may prefer to use it for personal needs. But this does not affect the principles of profit measurement. Suppose that *A* had shown in his balance sheet the loss in value of his taxi, but had still withdrawn for personal use an annual cash sum of £657. Compare the balance sheet at the end of the first year with that in which no depreciation calculation was made:

	(I)		(II)		
	No depreciation		*With depreciation*		
	£			£	£
Taxi	950	Taxi			
Cash	50	Cost		950	
		Depreciation		120	
				—	830
		Cash			50
	1,000				880
Loan	400	Loan			400
Capital	600	Capital			480
	1,000				880

The cash is the same in both cases; but while (I) shows the taxi at its original cost, and suggests that the ownership claim is still £600, (II) shows the depreciated value of the taxi and indicates clearly that *A* has taken out of the business not only all the profit but also some of his original invested capital.

We must not suggest that the depreciation *provision*, as it is usually called, is a very precise measurement of the loss in value of an asset. In practice its estimation and interpretation are fraught with difficulties. This, however, is well known. To omit depreciation altogether would be to suggest that no economic change had occurred with respect to the asset concerned. A reasonable approximation, based on known assumptions, is usually better than no information at all.

It should be noted that in practice the single asset 'cash' that we have shown in this simplified example would probably be represented by a set of current assets and liabilities, and the taxi by a collection of different fixed assets.

Although what follows is not directly relevant to depreciation or profit measurement, it should also be noted (since the example we have used may otherwise mislead) that it would usually be a waste of resources from the business owner's point of view to accumulate in the business a cash balance that would not be required for the replacement of assets for some years; it would be normal to use the available cash in the interval to expand the earning power of the business, for example by acquiring additional stock in trade or fixed assets, or both, or possibly by investing in other businesses. When the time came for the replacement of fixed assets the fact that the business had expanded and presumably become more profitable (and therefore more valuable) would make it correspondingly easier to raise additional finance from outside, e.g. in the form of an additional loan, the interest on which could be met out of the cash flow arising from the additional profit. Or the owner might invest more capital. There are many other financing possibilities, such as the repayment of loans by using funds not needed for the time being, with the intention of borrowing again when finance is needed for replacement or expansion at some later date. The function of the depreciation calculation is to show the amount needed to replace the *funds invested* in the asset, not the asset itself, which may not be replaced by a similar asset or even at all.

The annual reduction in the value of fixed assets which we call depreciation has no short run effect on the business liquidity; hence the failure to make, and record, a reasonable estimate of depreciation may not become apparent for a relatively long period, during which shareholders and other owners, and long-term creditors may be seriously deceived. When considering the changing liquidity of a business it is therefore useful to look at the figure of profit *before* deduction of depreciation, as shown in the second funds statement above. The sum of net profit and depreciation is often called the *cash flow* of the business. It would be better, however, to describe it as the *flow of working capital*, as usually it is not attributable only to changes in cash.

Intangible assets

In addition to fixed assets like land, buildings, vehicles, plant, machinery and equipment, which are called *tangible assets* because they are physical objects, there are so-called *intangible assets*. These fall into two distinct classes, *goodwill* and *others*.

Goodwill

If the value of the ownership interest recorded in the accounts is greater than (*a*) the sum of the values set upon those assets that could be sold or otherwise disposed of individually, *less* (*b*) the sum of the outside liabilities, we are left with a residue. We attribute this residual value to an asset called *goodwill*.

For example, suppose that a company spends £1,000,000 in buying a business as a going concern. The directors of the company assess at £900,000 the total value to be set on fixed and current assets which could have been bought separately. Suppose also that the liabilities taken over are £200,000. We then say that the *net tangible assets* are £700,000 and the goodwill is £300,000.

Where goodwill exists it may be regarded as the value of 'organization' – of the fact that a business is an organic whole, distinct from its separate parts, just as a person is more than the chemical elements that compose his or her body. In a well-organized business, contacts and understanding will have been created, among those who work in it, and between them and its suppliers and customers. A pool of knowledge of how best to get things done will have been formed. Such a business is likely to produce a greater flow of benefits and therefore to be worth more than the amount which would be received if the business came to an end, the assets that could be disposed of separately were all sold, and the liabilities were all paid off; and it is also likely to be more valuable than the sum of the amounts that would be needed to replace the same net assets.

So the estimation of the value of goodwill requires the estimation of the value of the business as a whole, as a going concern. Such an estimation is thought to be too subjective and uncertain for goodwill to be recorded in the accounts except where there is evidence of its value in the form of an actual purchase. It is therefore standard practice to record only 'purchased goodwill' in the accounts.

There is indeed a strong school of thought which considers that even purchased goodwill should be 'written out' of the books at once, as a debit to reserves. Where the reserves were insufficient these accountants would show any residue of goodwill in the balance sheet as a deduction from share capital.

In certain countries it is the practice to write off (depreciate) any purchased goodwill within a stated number of years. In the German Federal Republic the period is five years. In the United States the period is forty years. At the time of writing it appears that the German rule may be adopted for all member states of the EEC.

Other intangible assets

The 'non-goodwill' intangibles are assets from which benefits are expected over a number of years following the time of acquisition but which have no physical existence – literally that cannot be touched by the hand. They include such items as patents; knowledge confined to the business which has been built up inside it, for example from research and development; trade marks; and benefits expected to accrue from large advertising campaigns. The right to enjoy the benefits derived from such things can be sold, so that, unlike goodwill, these assets are separable from the business as a going concern.

From an economic or financial viewpoint the essential difference between intangible and tangible assets is that (*a*) generally speaking there is greater uncertainty about the size, duration and pattern of the expected flow of benefits from an intangible, and (*b*) if the flow of benefits of an intangible turns out to be zero, its realizable value is likely also to be zero because it has no alternative uses to anyone, whereas tangible assets often have alternative uses which give them a residual value, even if only as scrap.

This suggests, however, that the distinction between tangibles and intangibles can be over-emphasized, because value depends, not upon such physical characteristics as non-touchability, but upon economic characteristics. Some tangible assets also have no alternative use. For example, a specialized chemical plant built to produce a new product that turns out to be unsaleable may have to be scrapped and may have no residual value after the costs of demolition and clearing the site have been met. Worse, it may have a negative value because of the cost of clearing the site (and perhaps eradicating noxious residues).

Under historical cost accounting, the approach to the valuation of intangible assets is strongly influenced by prudence. So far as they have been bought outside the business, as may be the case with patents, they will be entered in the accounts at cost and reduced in value by annual debits to profit and loss (depreciation) over their commercial life (which may be limited by their legal life, as with patents). Where the intangible asset has been created inside the business, e.g. by research and development, standard practice calls for stringent tests as to the reality of the expected benefits before a value is set upon it: if these tests cannot be satisfied the whole expenditure is written off at once to profit and loss.

Trade investments

Trade investments is a convenient term for investments which are intended to be held indefinitely or for a long period in order to provide continuing income or other, indirect, benefits. They are distinguished from investments that are current assets – made in order to earn a temporary return on cash that will shortly be needed for other purposes or that is held to meet contingencies. For instance, a company making a product from woven cloth might decide, as part of its business policy, to hold as a trade investment shares in a company from which it obtained its cloth.

Trade investments are sometimes regarded as neither 'fixed' nor 'current'. This is because investments in other businesses will themselves usually have both types of asset, so that an investment in them can be regarded as a mixture of both. They are categorized as fixed investments by those who prefer to have only two classes of asset: current or fixed.

Trade investments are normally valued at their historical cost but they are written down to a lower value if it is clear that the future benefits no longer justify that figure, the loss being charged to profit and loss account. If they are 'listed' – i.e. if they have a stock exchange quotation – a valuation on the basis of this is recorded in a footnote, but is not necessarily taken as an indication of their value on a longer-term view.

In company accounts special treatment is given to two types of trade investment, investments in *subsidiary companies* and investments in *associated companies*. Subsidiary companies are those effectively controlled by the company under consideration, which normally owns more than half their ordinary share capital – commonly all of it. Associated companies are not under full control, but the owning company has a substantial say in their management and has a significant share holding. Both kinds of investment are separately classified in the balance sheet. Where there are subsidiary companies, a second, *consolidated balance sheet*, and a *consolidated profit and loss account*, are usually prepared; these can be regarded as the result of adding together, with certain adjustments, the individual accounts of all the companies in a group, a group consisting of a *holding* or *parent* company, and all its subsidiary companies. For further information on these matters, as on company accounting procedures generally, reference should be made to texts on company accounts.

Fictitious assets

Balance sheets sometimes contain, among the assets, items that some accountants would prefer to regard as deductions in the claims part of the balance sheet. (Arithmetically, a positive item among assets is of course equivalent to a negative one among claims.) These are sometimes called *fictitious assets*. They include such items as: losses – debit balances on profit and loss account; *preliminary* or *formation* expenses – amounts spent in the process of setting up a company; *new issue expenses* – costs of raising money by issuing shares. All these, if not written off against reserves, could be reasonably shown in the balance sheet as deductions from the ownership interest. Another fictitious asset is *discount on debentures* – the difference between (*a*) the nominal or face value of a long-term loan to the company and (*b*) the amount of cash actually raised when the loan is issued where this amount is smaller than face value. When such loans fall due they are usually repaid at their face value (sometimes rather above this), so that the initial difference or 'discount' is in effect deferred interest on the loan. It can be argued that it is appropriate when the loan is first issued to deduct this discount from the liability shown* and then gradually to increase the liability (with corresponding debits to profit) over the life of the loan until, at the due date, the full amount repayable is shown. In practice, however, it is usual to write the discount off at once. In so far as this is not done the difference (which has of course to be brought in somehow to make the books balance) may be shown as a 'fictitious asset' instead of as a deduction from the liability.

Capital expenditure

Tangible and intangible fixed assets can be bought, or they can be created inside the business. Outlays to purchase or create them are called collectively *capital expenditure*. Here the word 'capital' is being used in a special sense, namely to indicate the relatively long-term nature of the flow of benefits expected to be obtained from the outlay. From a book-keeping point of view, capital expenditure is (*a*) a fall in cash or some other asset (or a rise in liability to creditors) coupled with (*b*) a corresponding rise in a new fixed asset.

* Thus showing in the balance sheet the 'discounted present value' of the liability.

Capital expenditure is distinguished by its name from *revenue expenditure* (better described perhaps as *current expenditure*) which is expenditure on the acquisition of current assets or made to secure some other benefit which will expire rapidly (such as the benefit from the payment of rent), usually within a single annual accounting period. In this context the words 'capital' and 'revenue' are both used as adjectives to convey the sense respectively of extended duration and short duration.

9 Problems in double entry and final accounts

Introduction

The basic principles have now been covered. In this chapter we shall work through a number of examples to illustrate applications of these principles. When working through the examples, one should tick off each item in the list of data given, noting how it is entered in the accounts; at the same time one should tick the relevant item in the solution. Similarly one should note how the totals and balances are obtained in the solution, and should check the transfers between accounts, again ticking each debit against its corresponding credit. Finally one should check the figures in the 'final accounts' – the accounting reports in the form of profit and loss accounts, balance sheets, and so on – against the double entry records from which they are obtained. It is good practice to work out the exercise for oneself before looking at the solution.

In some of the examples the double entry analysis given represents what would be in practice the accounting records of the relevant business; in others it is the working method by which a particular report or estimate is obtained on 'working papers', the problem being such that the business's main accounting records would not necessarily be affected.

Example 1

Record the following transactions, relating to the business of a trader, X, in double entry form, using schematic T accounts.

Jan 1 (a) X starts the business by paying £600 from his private funds into the business bank account.
   6 (b) Wages paid by drawing cash from bank, £20.
   6 (c) Fittings (to be treated as fixed assets) bought and paid for by cheque, £32.
   8 (d) Goods for stock bought from S Ltd on credit, £516.

10   (*e*) Goods sold to *Z* on credit, £206. (Note: as we are not told
the cost of sales, this has to be worked out – see *l* below.)

12   (*f*) *S* Ltd is paid in full by cheque.

13   (*g*) Goods are sold for cash, which is paid into the bank, £116.

14   (*h*) One month's rent is paid, by cheque, £40.

19   (*i*) *Z* pays in full. The money is paid into the bank.

20   (*j*) Goods are sold to *Y* on credit, £86.

31   (*k*) The business's debt for electricity supplied during the month
is recorded, £5.

(*l*) The stock remaining is valued at £311. The difference between
this and the stock bought is recorded as cost of sales.

(*m*) The month's depreciation of fittings is estimated as 10 per cent
of cost.

Prove the accuracy of your work by listing, in debit and credit columns, the balances on the ledger accounts, that is, by drawing up a trial balance as at the end of January. You are not asked to prepare a profit and loss account or a balance sheet.

The solution of this problem is given opposite. The cost of sales is found by subtracting the closing stock valuation of £311 from the amount of stock bought during the month, £516. The £311 is then the closing balance of stock. In businesses in which no continuous stock record is kept the cost of sales can only be found in this way.

The depreciation of fittings is 10 per cent of £32, that is £3 to the nearest £. In the solution we show the balance of the fittings account as reduced by this amount. It is often convenient, however, to use a second account in which the amount of depreciation to be deducted from an asset (the depreciation provision) is accumulated as a credit balance, a kind of negative asset, so that the net balance sheet value of the asset is obtained as the difference between the debit balance on the asset account and the credit balance on the depreciation *provision* account. (The latter is to be distinguished from the account that shows the debit for the depreciation *expense* which will be transferred to the profit and loss account.)

Note that in this example we are recording individual debtors and creditors as distinct from the totals of trade debtors and trade creditors in previous examples. In small businesses it may be possible to dispense with total accounts. In most businesses, however, there are so many debtors and creditors that it is essential to use total accounts. We shall discuss in Chapter 10 how the record of individual debts and liabilities is linked up with the total accounts. The solution is as follows:

Bank			
	£		£
(*a*) Capital	600	(*b*) Wages	20
(*g*) Sales	116	(*c*) Fittings	32
(*i*) Z	206	(*f*) S Ltd	516
		(*h*) Rent	40
		Balance c/d	314
	922		922
Balance b/d	314		

Capital		
		£
	(*a*) Bank	600

Wages	
	£
(*b*) Bank	20

Fittings			
	£		£
(*c*) Bank	32	(*m*) Depreciation	3
		Balance c/d	29
	32		32
Balance b/d	29		

Stock			
	£		£
(*d*) S Ltd	516	(*l*) Cost of sales	205
		Balance c/d	311
	516		516
Balance b/d	311		

S Ltd			
	£		£
(*f*) Bank	516	(*d*) Stock	516

Sales			
			£
		(*e*) Z	206
		(*g*) Bank	116
		(*j*) Y	86
			408

Z			
	£		£
(*e*) Sales	206	(*i*) Bank	206

Rent	
	£
(*h*) Bank	40

Y		
	£	£
(*j*) Sales	86	

Electricity	
	£
(*k*) El. Bd.	5

Electricity Board		
		£
	(*k*) Electricity	5

Cost of sales	
	£
(*l*) Stock	205

Depreciation (expense)	
	£
(*m*) Fittings	3

Trial balance, 31 January

	£	£
Bank	314	
Capital		600
Wages	20	
Fittings	29	
Stock	311	
Sales		408
Rent	40	
Y (debtor)	86	
Electricity	5	
Electricity Board (creditor)		5
Cost of sales	205	
Depreciation (expense)	3	
	1,013	1,013

Example 2

Use the results of Example 1. Transfer the balances on the sales and cost of sales accounts to a trading account, and obtain the gross profit as a balance.

Transfer the gross profit, and the balances on the expense accounts, to a profit and loss account, and obtain the net profit as a balance.

Transfer the net profit to the capital account.

Prepare a new trial balance.

Using the figures in the relevant ledger accounts draft a trading and a profit and loss account and a balance sheet as at 31 January, in a form suitable for report to the owner.

In this example we have distinguished between the *trading account* (showing sales, cost of sales and, as a balance, gross profit) and the *profit and loss account*. This distinction is now tending to become obsolete; what is here distinguished as the trading account is just as likely to be merged in the profit and loss account. However, the old form is still sometimes used.

In the solution that follows only the accounts that are changed are shown; the others remain as in the solution of Example 1.

First we have the double entry accounts:

Trading account

	£		£
Cost of sales	205	Sales	408
Gross profit			
transferred	203		—
	408		408

Profit and loss account

	£		£
Rent	40	Gross profit	
Wages	20	transferred	203
Electricity	5		
Depreciation	3		
Balance c/d	135		—
	203		203
Net profit		Balance b/d	135
transferred			
to Capital	135		

Capital

	£		£
Balance c/d	735	Balance b/d	600
		Profit and	
		loss	135
	735		735
		Balance b/d	735

Sales

	£		£
Trading	408	Balance b/d	408

Cost of sales

	£		£
Balance b/d	205	Trading	205

Rent

	£		£
Balance b/d	40	Profit and	
		loss	40

Wages

	£		£
Balance b/d	20	Profit and	
		loss	20

Electricity

	£		£
Balance b/d	5	Profit and loss	5

Depreciation (*expense*)

	£		£
Balance b/d	3	Profit and loss	3

Trial balance, 31 January (after closing entries)

		£	£
Capital			735
Bank	(as in Example 1)	314	
Fittings	,, ,, ,, ,,	29	
Stock	,, ,, ,, ,,	311	
Debtor (Y)	,, ,, ,, ,,	86	
Creditor (Electricity Board)	,, ,, ,, ,,		5
		740	740

D

The reports to the owner are as follows:

*Trading and profit and loss account
January 19—*

		£	£
	Sales		408
less	Cost of sales		205
	Gross profit		203
less	Rent	40	
	Wages	20	
	Electricity	5	
	Depreciation	3	
		—	68
	Net profit		135

Balance sheet, 31 January 19—

	£	£
Fittings at cost *less* depreciation		29
Stock	311	
Trade debtor	86	
Cash at bank	314	
	—	711
		740
Capital		
Balance 1 January	600	
Profit for January	135	
	—	735
Creditor for expenses		5
		740

The form of these final accounts, and of those given in the following examples, should be noted. In particular note the division of the assets in the balance sheet into the two groups of fixed and current assets, and the order in which the assets are listed. It is usual when drafting a balance sheet to 'marshal' assets in either decreasing or increasing order of liquidity, so that the most liquid, cash, comes last (or first). In fact it is not always easy to say whether one asset is more liquid than another. There has developed, however, a fairly standard conventional 'order of liquidity' which we shall follow here: it is convenient to follow standard practice in this respect, as this makes accounting reports easier to read.

Similarly, current liabilities (those due for payment within about a year) are grouped separately from others, and there is a tendency to list the liabilities in the order in which they are due for payment.

Example 3

From the following trial balance as at 31 March 19x2, taken from the ledger of *A*, a trader, prepare final accounts for the financial year to 31 March 19x2:

	£	£
Capital, 1 April 19x1		1,600
Sales		5,900
Cost of sales	3,220	
Stock, 31 March 19x2	510	
Rent	100	
Returns inward	160	
Cash discounts allowed	150	
Cash discounts received		190
Drawings	581	
Furniture and fittings at cost	580	
Depreciation (provision)		160
,, (expense)	29	
Bank	240	
Salaries	1,100	
General expenses, including lighting and heating, insurance, postage, and telephone	180	
Debtors	2,300	
Creditors		1,300
	9,150	9,150

Certain of the terms given above are new. Their meanings are as follows:

1 *Returns inward:* this debit is to be treated as a reduction in the sales; it represents the cancellation of certain sales by return of the goods. (The closing stock given must be assumed to include the goods sent back.)

2 *Cash discounts allowed:* this debit is the counterpart of a credit or credits to debtors accounts. A percentage allowance is often made to a debtor if he pays before the end of a given time period and his

account is credited with this. The corresponding debit represents a financial expense.*

3 *Cash discounts received:* here it is the creditors whose claims have been reduced for a similar reason. The credit is, therefore, a financial gain.

4 *Depreciation provision:* this was explained in Example 1. It is an offset to the corresponding asset account.

The ledger accounts will be as follows:

Capital				Sales			
	£		£		£		£
Drawings	581	Balance b/d	1,600	Profit and		Balance	
Balance c/d	2,170	Profit and		loss	5,900	b/d	5,900
		loss	1,151				
	2,751		2,751				
		Balance b/d	2,170				

Cost of sales				Stock		
	£		£		£	
Balance		Profit and		Balance b/d	510	
b/d	3,220	loss	3,220			

Rent				Returns inward			
	£		£		£		£
Balance b/d	100	Profit and		Balance b/d	160	Profit and	
		loss	100			loss	160

Cash discounts allowed				Cash discounts received			
	£		£		£		£
Balance b/d	150	Profit and		Profit and		Balance b/d	190
		loss	150	loss	190		

Drawings				Furniture and fittings		
	£		£		£	
Balance b/d	581	Capital	581	Balance b/d	580	

Depreciation provision				Depreciation (expense)			
			£		£		£
		Balance b/d	160	Balance b/d	29	Profit and	
						loss	29

* Earlier payment of debts may save interest on a bank overdraft; in any case it gives the enterprise additional finance.

Bank		
	£	
Balance b/d	240	

Salaries		
	£	£
Balance b/d	1,100	Profit and loss 1,100

General expenses		
	£	£
Balance b/d	180	Profit and loss 180

Debtors		
	£	
Balance b/d	2,300	

Creditors	
	£
Balance b/d	1,300

Trading and profit and loss account

	£		£
Returns	160	Sales	5,900
Cost of sales	3,220		
Gross profit c/d	2,520		
	5,900		5,900
Rent	100	Gross profit b/d	2,520
Salaries	1,100	Discounts received	190
General expenses	180		
Depreciation	29		
Discounts allowed	150		
Balance, net profit transferred to capital	1,151		
	2,710		2,710

Final trial balance

	£	£
Capital		2,170
Stock	510	
Furniture and fittings	580	
Depreciation		160
Bank	240	
Debtors	2,300	
Creditors		1,300
	3,630	3,630

The reports can now be drafted, and will appear as set out below. We have shown all the ledger accounts in order to give a complete picture. If the problem was merely to prepare accounting reports (as distinct from showing the entries in *A*'s books too) it is clear that we could have worked directly from the original trial balance, copying out only such ledger accounts as were needed to check any adjustments to be made to the figures: in this particular example we could have prepared the final accounting reports directly from the original data.

Until, however, one has the confidence that goes with complete understanding and a good deal of practice, it is probably better to write down the ledger accounts as a first step in the solution, since this, though slower, takes one back to first principles.

The 'narrative' or 'columnar' form of presentation for accounting reports used below and in previous examples in this book is usually easier for laymen to understand than the T form, and facilitates the comparison of the results of successive periods. On the other hand, the T form sometimes economizes space; and is probably quicker to read if one understands accounts. It is still used sometimes for the presentation of reports, as shown in Example 5.

A
Trading and profit and loss account
Year to 31 March 19x2

		£	£
	Sales *less* returns		5,740
less	Cost of sales		3,220
	Gross profit		2,520
	Discounts received		190
			2,710
less	Rent	100	
	Salaries	1,100	
	Lighting, heating, insurance, postage, and sundries	180	
	Depreciation	29	
	Discounts allowed	150	
			1,559
	Net profit for year as shown in balance sheet		1,151

Balance sheet at 31 March 19x2

		£
	Fixed asset	
	Furniture and fittings at cost	580
less	Depreciation	160
		420

Current assets		
Stock	510	
Debtors	2,300	
Cash at bank	240	
	3,050	
less Current liabilities		
Creditors	1,300	
	——	1,750
Net assets		2,170
Represented by capital		
Balance at 1 April 19x1		1,600
Profit for year to 31 March 19x2		1,151
		2,751
less Drawings for year to 31 March 19x2		581
Balance at 31 March 19x2		2,170

Example 4

The trial balance below has been taken from the books of *AB*, a wholesale trader. From this trial balance prepare final accounts (trading and profit and loss account and balance sheet) for the year to 31 December, in a form suitable for presentation to the management, taking into account the additional information provided. You are not required to show the closing entries in the books.

Trial balance, 31 December

	£	£
Stock	1,700	
Sales		10,932
Trade debtors	1,124	
Trade creditors		782
Furniture and equipment (original cost)	1,560	
Depreciation provision		496
Returns	62	
Salaries	1,300	
Bad debts provision		24
General expenses	948	
Cost of sales	7,063	
Cash at bank	362	
Cash in hand (petty cash)	25	
Drawings	510	
Capital (as at 1 January)		2,420
	14,654	14,654

At the end of the year the following matters had not been recorded in the books:

(*a*) Salaries accrued due but unpaid amounted to £15.
(*b*) Depreciation on furniture and equipment for the year is to be at the rate of 10 per cent per annum on original cost.
(*c*) The trade debtors balance included £24 considered irrecoverable.
(*d*) A general bad debts provision is to be made, equal to 5 per cent of the debtors balance in the balance sheet before deduction of the general provision.

Before we tackle the problem, some explanation is necessary of items (*c*) and (*d*) above. When a debt becomes irrecoverable or finally 'bad' it is 'written off as a bad debt'. This means that the total of the debtors is reduced by a credit entry equal to the amount lost, and a corresponding debit is made to an expense account called *bad debts*, or sometimes *bad and doubtful debts*.

Sometimes when a debt or part of a debt is of doubtful value, but not finally known to be bad, the total of debtors is not reduced (which means that the amount written off will be lost sight of), but instead the amount that is doubtful is credited to a *bad debts provision account*, as, in effect, a negative asset; this is shown in the balance sheet as a deduction from debtors; the corresponding debit entry again is made in the bad debts expense account.

Often statistical evidence shows that in a given business a certain proportion of all debts incurred in a given period will probably prove bad, though it is not known which particular debts will lose their value. In such cases a *general provision* for bad debts is made each year, as a given percentage of the balance sheet value of all debts; this provision is deducted from the total of debtors in preparing the balance sheet. The accounting entries are the same as for the specific provision described in the preceding paragraph.

When a bad debts provision exists, such debts as prove finally bad, and have not been written off earlier, are eliminated by crediting debtors account and debiting the provision account.

It is important to develop a procedure that will enable problems of this type, where adjustments to the trial balance are necessary, to be tackled surely and swiftly without undue risk of error. The following paragraphs sketch out such a procedure.

Decide which items in the trial balance (TB) are to be adjusted. Open up T accounts for these in your working papers, inserting in the T accounts the balances from the TB, ticking the latter off as this is done. Make the adjustments in the T accounts, taking care always to match debits and credits, ticking off each adjustment required in the list of original information as it is made. The final balances on the T accounts, together with the remaining (unticked) TB balances, give the figures for the final accounts. As each figure is entered in the profit and loss account or the balance sheet, tick it in the TB or the relevant T account.

If you prefer you can prepare a new TB from the balances in the old TB and in the T accounts, before preparing the final accounts.

Once you are fairly sure of yourself, it is a waste of time to open up T accounts for any balances not to be amended: these can be picked up directly from the TB when you prepare the final accounts.

As you develop facility, you will probably find that, for simple adjustments, you can amend the TB directly and omit the T accounts.

It is often best to draw up a rough profit and loss account and balance sheet in the first place and from these prepare the fair copy.

Never allow debits and credits to be out of balance. Whenever you record a debit, record at the same time a corresponding credit, or vice versa.

We shall show here only the ledger accounts that record salaries and the liability for accrued salaries, depreciation expense and depreciation provision, trade debtors, bad debts expense and bad debts provision. The accounts in question are:

Salaries (expense)		*Salaries* *(liability for amounts accrued)*	
£			£
Balance b/d 1,300		Salaries	
Liability for		(expense) 15	
amounts			
accrued 15			
1,315			

Depreciation (*expense*)		Depreciation provision	
£			£
Depreciation provision 156		Balance b/d 496	
		Depreciation expense 156	
		652	

Trade debtors		Bad debts provision	
£	£	£	£
Balance b/d 1,124	Bad debts provision 24	Trade debtors 24	Balance b/d 24
	Balance c/d 1,100	Balance c/d 55	Bad debts expense 55
1,124	1,124	79	79
Balance b/d 1,100			Balance b/d 55*

Bad debts expense	
£	
Bad debts provision 55	

* This is 5 per cent of £1,100.

The final reports are as follows:

AB
Trading and profit and loss account
Year to 31 December 19—

	£	£
Sales *less* returns		10,870
less Cost of sales		7,063
		3,807
less Salaries	1,315	
General expenses	948	
Depreciation	156	
Bad debts	55	
		2,474
Net profit		1,333

Balance sheet, 31 December 19—

	£	£
Furniture and equipment		
Cost	1,560	
less Depreciation	652	
	——	908
Current assets		
Stock	1,700	
Trade debtors	1,045*	
Cash at bank and in hand	387	
	——	3,132
		4,040
less Current liabilities		
Trade creditors	782	
Accrued expenses	15	
	——	797
Net assets		3,243
Capital		
Balance, 1 January 19—		2,420
Profit for year		1,333
		3,753
less Drawings		510
Balance, 31 December 19—		3,243

* £1,100−£55=£1,045.

When a large number of adjustments have to be made, a columnar method may be found more convenient than T accounts (though sketching in T account entries on scrap paper may still be helpful in thinking out the debit and credit entries for a particular transaction). The working figures for Exercise 4 are shown below as they would appear in columnar form. The first two columns contain the debit and credit items of the original TB. The second two columns contain the adjustments. The third two give the profit and loss figures that result from combining the profit and loss items in the first two sets of columns. The final two columns similarly give the balance sheet figures from combining the balance sheet items in the first two sets of columns. The balancing debit item in the profit and loss columns is the profit. When inserted on the credit side of the balance sheet columns, the latter also balance. The final two sets of columns thus only require rearrangement for the final reports.

Columnar worksheet for Exercise 4

	Balances in books		Adjustments		Profit and loss items		Balance sheet items	
£	Dr	Cr	Dr	Cr	Dr	Cr	Dr	Cr
Stock	1,700						1,700	
Sales		10,932				10,932		
Trade debtors	1,124						1,100	
Trade creditors		782		24(c)				782
Furniture and equipment (cost)	1,560						1,560	
Depreciation (provision)		496		156(b)				652
Depreciation (expense)			156(b)		156			
Returns	62				62			
Salaries (expense)	1,300		15(a)		1,315			
Salaries (accrued)				15(a)				15
Bad debts (provision)		24	24(c)	55(d)				55
Bad debts (expense)			55(d)		55			
General expenses	948				948			
Cost of sales	7,063				7,063			
Cash at bank	362						362	
Cash in hand	25						25	
Drawings	510						510	
Capital		2,420						2,420
Profit and loss					1,333			1,333
	14,654	14,654	250	250	10,932	10,932	5,257	5,257

Example 5

From the following trial balance of the *XY* Club, and the other information provided, prepare the club's final accounts (income and expenditure account* and balance sheet) for the year to 31 December 19—:

	£	£
Surplus, 1 January†		750
Investments at cost	560	
Cash at bank	56	
Petty cash	16	
Stock of unsold journals, 1 January, at cost	130	
Interest on investments		23
Subscriptions		470
Salary of secretary	400	
Stationery, postage, etc.	31	
Rent	60	
Printing expenses of journal for year 19—	85	
Sale of journals		95
	1,338	1,338

The following matters have not yet been recorded in the accounts and are therefore not reflected in the trial balance figures:

(*a*) The market value of investments at 31 December was £520. The book value is not to be altered, but the market value is to be noted on the balance sheet. (This is the normal practice.)

(*b*) Of the stock of journals, including those printed during the year, copies valued in the books at their cost of £90 were sold during the year. (Show the net profit or loss from the journal for the year as a single item in the account, with revenue and cost of sales inset.)

(*c*) At 31 December, rent of £20 was owing for the last quarter of the year.

(*d*) At 31 December, subscriptions for the year still unpaid amounted to £30.

Closing entries in the books are not required.

* *Income and expenditure account* is used instead of *profit and loss account* for non-profit-making enterprises.

† This is equivalent to the capital account of the sole trader. It measures the surplus of assets over liabilities – the accumulated 'wealth' of the club to date.

Here we have to apply our principles to a new form of organization. This should cause no serious trouble if we know the principles thoroughly. Calculate the effect of the adjustments necessitated by (*b*), (*c*) and (*d*) by using T accounts (ticking off the opening balances for these in the trial balance and obtaining new balances on these accounts) and prepare a new rough trial balance *after* the adjustments to prove your arithmetic. The printing expenses should be transferred to the stock account as an increase in the balance sheet value of the journals. The adjustment for cost of sales can then be made. Then prepare the income and expenditure account exactly as you would a profit and loss account. (There is no trading section in the usual sense, though the section showing the financial results of the publishing of the journal is a kind of trading account.) Add the surplus ('profit') or deduct the deficit ('loss') for the year to or from the opening surplus in the balance sheet to arrive at the final surplus or deficit.

The ledger account form of report presentation has been used here for illustrative purposes. In practice, however, it would usually be better to use the more easily understood narrative (columnar) form of previous examples.

The solution is as follows:

Adjustments:

(*b*)　　　**Stock of journals**

	£		£
Balance b/d	130	Transfer to	
Expenses	85	cost of	
		sales	90
		Balance c/d	125
	215		215
Balance b/d	125		

Journal expenses

	£		£
Balance b/d	85	Transfer to	
		stock	85

Journals: cost of sales

	£	
Transfer from		
stock	90	

(*c*)　　　**Rent (expense)**

	£
Balance b/d	60
Liability	20
	80

Rent (liability)

		£
	Expense	20

(d) *Subscriptions (revenue)*   *Subscriptions (debtors)*

	£		£
Balance b/d	470	Subscription	
Debtors	30	revenue	30
	500		

Final accounts:

XY Club
Income and expenditure account
Year to 31 December 19—

	£		£	£
Salary of secretary	400	Subscriptions		500
Rent	80	Investment income		23
Stationery, postage, etc.	31	Sale of journals	95	
Surplus for year	17*	*less* Cost of sales	90	
				5
	528			528

Balance sheet, 31 December 19—

	£			£
Rent due		20	Petty cash	16
Surplus			Cash at bank	56
Balance 1 January	750		Investments at cost	
Surplus for year	17		(market value at	
	—	767	31 December 19—, £520)	560
			Debtors for subscriptions	30
			Stock of journals at cost	125
		787		787

Example 6

The following estimated data relate to a manufacturing business which is to begin operations on 1 January 19—. You are required to show how much money must be paid in by the owners as capital in order to finance the business until the following 31 March. Show also the profit and loss calculation. Prove your work by constructing

---

* This is the balance. In reports (as distinct from the ledger accounts themselves) it is not usual to show the 'brought-down' part of the profit balance below the line when the 'ledger account form' is used.

the balance sheet at 31 March 19—. The management have decided
that for this purpose work in progress and finished goods are to be
valued at direct cost.

Data:	£
Fixed assets to be bought and paid for in January	
Freehold factory	4,000
Machinery and equipment	10,000
Furniture, fittings, etc.	2,500
Motor vehicles	3,000
Raw materials bought	
February (to be paid for in March)	1,000
March (to be paid for in April)	2,000
Wages of operatives engaged on production, to be treated as part of the value of work in progress	
February	800
March	1,200
Salaries, non-manufacturing wages, and other expenses	
January	200
February	300
March	300
Balance sheet value (cost) of raw material used for production	
February	400
March	600
Balance sheet value (direct cost) of finished goods produced	
March	2,300
Balance sheet value (direct cost) of finished goods sold	
March	1,800
Sales value of finished goods sold	
March (to be paid for in April)	2,800
Cash balance at bank at 31 March is required to be at least	1,500

Depreciation on the fixed assets (factory, machinery, equipment,
furniture, fittings, and motor vehicles) can be ignored.

Here we have a new type of problem. We are asked, now, not to
prepare a set of accounts for events that have taken place but to
forecast how the accounts will appear if certain events happen; that
is, to construct a *budget* based on the management forecast. However,
the principles that have been used for the first kind of problem can
be applied equally well to the second.

The problem is to ascertain the amount of cash to be paid in that will just leave a balance of £1,500 on 31 March. This can be found by first constructing a hypothetical cash account for the period on the assumption that the opening balance is zero and that any excess of payments over receipts can be treated as a bank overdraft. The cash needed to be paid in at the beginning will be equal to the highest level of credit balance (i.e. overdraft) shown on this hypothetical cash account during the period, *plus* the amount, if any, needed to bring the closing balance shown up to £1,500 debit. We can ignore depreciation as this does not involve a cash outlay.

We solve the problem here by constructing T accounts for the three months as working papers.

The solution is as follows:

Cash at bank

		£
Jan	Factory	4,000
,,	Machinery, etc.	10,000
,,	Furniture, etc.	2,500
,,	Motor vehicles	3,000
,,	Salaries, etc.	200
Feb	Work in progress (wages)	800
,,	Salaries, etc.	300
Mar	Work in progress (wages)	1,200
,,	Salaries, etc.	300
,,	Creditors	1,000
		23,300

Freehold factory

		£	
Jan	Bank	4,000	

Machinery and equipment

		£	
Jan	Bank	10,000	

Furniture, fittings, etc.

		£	
Jan	Bank	2,500	

Motor vehicles

		£	
Jan	Bank	3,000	

Raw materials

		£			£
Feb	Creditors	1,000	Feb	Work in progress	400
Mar	,,	2,000	Mar	,, ,, ,,	600
				Balance c/d	2,000
		3,000			3,000
	Balance b/d	2,000			

Salaries and non-manufacturing wages

		£	
Jan	Bank	200	
Feb	,,	300	
Mar	,,	300	
		800	

Work in progress

		£			£
Feb	Bank	800	Mar	Finished goods	2,300
,,	Raw materials	400			
Mar	,, ,,	600			
,,	Bank	1,200		Balance c/d	700
		3,000			3,000
	Balance b/d	700			

Finished goods

		£			£
Mar	Work in progress	2,300	Mar	Cost of sales	1,800
				Balance c/d	500
		2,300			2,300
	Balance b/d	500			

Cost of sales

	£	
Mar Finished goods	1,800	

Sales

			£
		Mar Debtors	2,800

Creditors

	£		£
Mar Bank	1,000	Feb Raw materials	1,000
Balance c/d	2,000	Mar ,, ,,	2,000
	3,000		3,000
		Balance b/d	2,000

Debtors

	£	
Mar Sales	2,800	

The cash at bank account shows by 31 March a credit balance (i.e. overdraft) of £23,300. That this is the maximum overdraft needed in the three months can be seen by inspection, as there have been no receipts.* As the required condition is a *debit* balance of at least £1,500, an additional debit of £23,300+£1,500=£24,800 is needed. This gives the answer. We can now debit cash at bank with £24,800 as at 1 January and credit capital with the same amount to give our final budgeted cash account. The final balances on these accounts are then:

Cash at bank			*Capital*	
	£			£
Balance			Balance	
b/d	1,500		b/d	24,800

* Had there been it would have been necessary to calculate the balance month by month (in practice perhaps even day by day).

A trial balance will now show:

	£	£
Cash at bank	1,500	
Capital		24,800
Factory	4,000	
Machinery, etc.	10,000	
Furniture, etc.	2,500	
Motor vehicles	3,000	
Raw materials	2,000	
Salaries, etc.	800	
Work in progress	700	
Finished goods	500	
Cost of sales	1,800	
Sales		2,800
Creditors		2,000
Debtors	2,800	
	29,600	29,600

The profit and loss budget will be:

	£
Sales	2,800
less Cost of sales	1,800
Gross profit	1,000
less General expenses	800
Net profit, subject to depreciation	200

The budgeted balance sheet will be:

	£			£
Capital to be paid in 1 January	24,800	Freehold factory at cost		4,000
Profit (before depreciation) for the three months to 31 March	200	Machinery and equipment at cost		10,000
	25,000	Furniture and fittings, etc., at cost		2,500
Creditors	2,000	Motor vehicles at cost		3,000
				19,500

			£
Stocks:			
Raw materials		2,000	
Work in progress		700	
Finished goods		500	
		3,200	
Debtors		2,800	
Cash at bank		1,500	
			7,500

27,000	27,000

As noted above, there is no need to provide depreciation, as we are only working out the cash position, and depreciation will not affect this. The balance sheet is provided to give an arithmetical check, and to give to management a general view of the asset and liability position.

The use of a direct cost valuation for work in progress and finished goods is not standard practice in company accounting reports, but it can be a useful simplifying convention in management reports. Its use affects the profit figure but not, of course, the flow of cash or the cash balance. The convention used must be borne in mind when the reports are interpreted.

Example 7

The accounting reports of clubs and similar bodies often take the form of a single receipts and payments account, that is, a statement in the form of a cash account that summarizes the cash receipts and payments under various heads. This may be quite informative and adequate for the purpose. Nevertheless, if there are other assets than cash, and also liabilities, these may have changed sufficiently in value to alter the financial position significantly: a receipts and payments account will not show this. An income and expenditure account, with a balance sheet, provides a fuller picture. An alternative to preparing these is to provide a list of assets and liabilities as an appendix to a receipts and payments account: this provides more information than the receipts and payments account, but does not show the net change in the value of assets *less* liabilities; and may become unwieldy if the organization's affairs are at all complicated. The following example shows how a receipts and payments account can be converted into a full set of final accounts on double entry principles.

The secretary of the ZZ Club has drafted the following receipts and payments account:

Year ended 31 December 19—

Receipts	£	Payments	£
Balance at bank,		Salaries and wages	876
1 January	522	Purchases of liquor	1,366
Subscriptions	896	Rent and rates	86
Sales of liquor	1,783	Light and heat	69
		Balance at bank,	
		31 December	804
	3,201		3,201

The following information is available:

1 Stock of liquor was valued at £233 at the beginning of the year and at £198 at the end.
2 The club owed £76 for purchases of liquor on 1 January and £87 at the end of the year.
3 The club owns equipment. This was valued at £186 on 1 January; the year's depreciation is set at £37.
4 The payments for light and heat include £7 for electricity for the last quarter of the previous year. The electricity bill for the final quarter of the year of the account has not been paid: it amounts to £12.

Prepare an income and expenditure (I & E) account for the year and the final balance sheet. Show the net trading results from liquor sales.

The first step in a problem of this kind is to establish the opening debit and credit position. This can be done by preparing an opening trial balance as at 1 January by listing assets and liabilities at that date and finding the opening surplus.

From the opening trial balance and the other data T accounts can be prepared for the period, on working papers. Then balances can be carried down and the final accounts prepared.

Note that here no T account need be prepared for cash: this is already provided in the question; all that is necessary is to complete the double entry by 'posting' each cash receipt or payment to the appropriate account.

Be careful to tick off items as a check on the completeness of the double entry: as the T accounts are opened tick off the balances entered in these against the items in the opening trial balance; tick off the cash balance in the opening TB against the opening balance in the receipts and payments summary; as the debit and credit aspect of the cash credits and debits are completed, tick the latter off in the receipts and payments summary; as the balance sheet is prepared tick off the items in the final TB.

Purchases of stock have to be derived by difference on the trade creditors account. This can be done because the opening and closing balances are known. Once purchases have been calculated, the contra debit in the stock account can be made. The cost of sales and the light and heat expense must similarly be found by difference. Note that here we use the light and heat expense account to record the amounts owing at the end of each period, dispensing with a separate account for the accrued liability.

These calculations are typical of what accountants call *incomplete record work*.

The opening trial balance is as follows:

	£	£
Cash	522	
Stock	233	
Trade creditors		76
Heat and light (accrued expense)		7
Equipment	186	
	941	83
Surplus (by difference)		858
	941	941

Double entry T accounts (except for cash, which is already given in the question) are as follows:

Stock

	£		£
Balance b/d	233	Cost of	
Creditors	1,377	sales	1,412*
		Balance	
		c/d	198
	1,610		1,610
Balance b/d	198		

Trade creditors

	£		£
Cash	1,366	Balance	
Balance c/d	87	b/d	76
		Stock	1,377*
	1,453		1,453
		Balance	
		b/d	87

Equipment

	£		£
Balance b/d	186	I & E (Depn)	37
		Balance c/d	149
	186		186
Balance b/d	149		

Light and heat

	£		£
Cash	69	Balance b/d	7
Balance c/d	12	I & E	74*
	81		81
		Balance b/d	12

* These figures are obtained by inserting the amount needed to make the two sides of the account balance after entering the balances carried down at the end of the year, which we are given.

Surplus

	£		£
		Balance b/d	858
		I & E	194
			1,052

Income and expenditure

	£		£
Salaries, etc.	876	Subscrip-	
Rent, etc.	86	tions	896
Light, etc.	74	Sales	1,783
Depreciation	37		
Cost of sales	1,412		
Surplus	194		
	2,679		2,679

Closing trial balance:

	£	£
Cash	804	
Stock	198	
Trade creditors		87
Heat and light (accrued expense)		12
Equipment	149	
Surplus		1,052
	1,151	1,151

In the above working solution the closing trial balance summarizes the balance sheet position after balancing the income and expenditure account. It is, of course, possible to prepare a trial balance before the income account is drafted; but here it hardly seems worth while.

It is also hardly worth while here opening separate T accounts for salaries, rent, and depreciation. These can be entered directly into the income and expenditure account, ticking them off in the receipts and payments account as this is done.

The final accounts as they might be presented to the club members are as follows:

ZZ Club
Income and expenditure account
Year ended 31 December 19—

	£		£	£
Salaries and wages	876	Subscriptions		896
Rent and rates	86	Profit on liquor		
Light and heat	74	sales:		
Depreciation	37	Sales	1,783	
Surplus for year	194	*less* Cost of sales	1,412	
				371
	1,267			1,267

Balance sheet at 31 December 19—

	£		£	£
Surplus		Equipment		149
Balance 1 January 19—	858	Stock of liquor	198	
Surplus for 19—	194	Cash at bank	804	
Balance 31 Dec 19—	1,052			1,002
	£			
Trade creditors	87			
Accrued expense	12			
	99			
	1,151			1,151

Example 8

Our next example is designed to give a further indication of the way in which accounting reports may be used. It calls for the preparation of an accounting report and for a discussion of the business significance of the figures in the report.

A business has the following balance sheet at the beginning of a given year:

	£		£	£
Capital	1,600	Equipment at		
		cost	1,600	
Creditors	400	*less* Depreciation	600	
				1,000
		Stock	500	
		Debtors	300	
		Cash	200	
				1,000
	2,000			2,000

The following forecasts are made of the trading results for the year:

	£
Sales	2,800
Purchases	2,000
Stock (valued at cost) at end of year	400
General expenses (all paid in cash)	1,100
Depreciation of equipment	200

The debtors at the end of the year for sales (included in the above sales figure) are estimated at £350.

The creditors at the end of the year for stock supplied (included in the above purchases figure) are estimated at £400.

The owner is not sure of the financial implications of these figures. He asks you, as accountant, whether you have any advice to offer him. He also tells you he does not intend to make any drawings during the year.

Advise the owner:

1 On the expected financial position, i.e. the position with respect to cash needs.
2 What special action, if any, this position calls for.

Analyse the year's expected transactions, using schematic double entry T accounts, and prepare a final balance sheet.

Cost of sales can be found by difference as the closing stock is known. The cash received from debtors and paid to creditors can be deduced in the same way, since the closing debtors and creditors are known.

Here again the T accounts would be working figures and would not be part of a formal set of records.

The solution is as follows. We have eliminated separate revenue and expense accounts from the working figures as redundant in this example: sales revenue, and expenses, are entered directly in the profit and loss account.

Cash

	£		£
Balance b/d	200	General	
Debtors	2,750	expenses	1,100
Balance c/d	150	Creditors	2,000
	3,100		3,100
		Balance b/d	150

Debtors

	£		£
Balance b/d	300	Cash	2,750
Profit and		Balance b/d	350
loss			
(sales)	2,800		
	3,100		3,100
Balance b/d	350		

Creditors

	£		£
Cash	2,000	Balance b/d	400
Balance c/d	400	Stock	2,000
	2,400		2,400
		Balance b/d	400

Stock

	£		£
Balance b/d	500	Profit and	
Creditors	2,000	loss	
		(cost of	
		sales)	2,100
		Balance c/d	400
	2,500		2,500
Balance b/d	400		

Capital

			£
		Balance b/d	1,600

Equipment

	£		£
Balance b/d	1,000	Profit and	
		loss	
		depre-	
		ciation)	200
		Balance c/d	800
	1,000		1,000
Balance b/d	800		

Profit and loss account

	£		£
Stock (cost of sales)	2,100	Debtors (sales)	2,800
Cash (general expenses)	1,100	Balance (loss) c/d	600
Equipment (depreciation)	200		
	3,400		3,400
Balance b/d	600		

Estimated balance sheet at 31 December 19—

	£	£		£	£
Capital 1 January	1,600		Equipment at		
less Loss for year	600		cost	1,600	
		1,000	*less* Depreciation	800	
Creditors	400				800
Bank overdraft			Stock	400	
(or other source			Debtors	350	
of finance)	150				750
	—	550			
		1,550			1,550

Estimated trading and profit and loss report
Year to 31 December 19—

	£	£
Sales		2,800
less Cost of sales		2,100
Gross profit		700
less General expenses	1,100	
Depreciation	200	
	—	1,300
Loss for year		600

There are two main points to be brought out:

1 *Profit and loss.* Unless gross profit can be increased considerably or expenses cut heavily it will be unprofitable to trade. Moreover, the economic loss may be greater than the accounts show if, as is presumably the case, the accounting expenses include nothing in respect of the owner's return on his invested capital or his services.

Suppose that the return required on the investment (that is, the return which, after allowing for differing risks, measures the best rate that could be earned by using the resources in other ways) is considered to be 10 per cent per annum, and that the balance sheet valuations are fairly good approximations to market value. Then the annual return required is about £160. Suppose also that the expenses already include a manager's salary and that the owner assesses his own remuneration for the general control of business policy (the 'entrepreneurial services') at £300 per annum. (We can assume that the business, being a small one, only consumes a small part of his time.) Then we can say that until the accounting profit reaches a level of £460 per annum £(160+300) there is no economic profit (assuming the other accounting figures, especially depreciation, are reasonably good measures of the economic costs).

2 *Finance*. It will not be possible to keep the business in operation unless additional external finance can be obtained, from the bank or elsewhere, of at least £150. (Presumably rather more may be needed to allow for contingencies and perhaps for fluctuations during the year; this could be dealt with, for example, by the granting of greater overdraft facilities by the bank.)

On a short-term view it is unlikely, however, that the owner will wish to put more money in, since the return before allowing for the cost of any additional finance is already negative. For the same reason it may not be easy to obtain finance from other sources even on loan; the figures suggest that the risk of default on interest and repayment is high.

On the other hand, it is not enough to consider only the short-term view. It may be worth while keeping the assets together in the expectation of better times later; and if so, it is likely that it will be worth while continuing to trade in order to maintain the organization as a whole, including its connections with suppliers and purchasers. (This is called 'maintaining the goodwill'.)

It is likely that some of the expenses, including depreciation, are unavoidable in the short run if the business is not to be closed, and to the extent that this is true they should be disregarded in computing the economic loss or gain from closing only temporarily. The same is true of the interest on capital and the owner's remuneration. This might lead us to the calculations below.

	A Long run	B Short run (one year)
	£	£
Expenses shown in accounts (other than cost of sales)*	1,300	1,300
Additional economic costs:		
Owner's remuneration, say	300	—
Interest on investment, say 10% on £1,600	160	—
	1,760	1,300
less Expenses shown in accounts that could not be saved by closing down for one year (such as rent, insurance, depreciation), let us say	—	500
Required contribution	1,760	800

* We assume that all these are costs that could be saved in the longer run if the business closed.

These suggest that (1) it is not worth while continuing in the long run unless the *contribution* to the overhead costs is expected to be at least £1,760; but (2) this year the overhead cost of keeping open, *provided that the business is to be continued thereafter* (so that the premises, etc., cannot be abandoned), is only £800 (presumably for wages, etc.). As the gross profit is £700, the net sacrifice from keeping open and trading this year, given the above decision, is only £100. This may be worth while incurring if it improves future prospects.

This brings out the very important point that economic costs must be considered *in relation to particular decisions*, and that special estimates may have to be made for each decision.

It must also be remembered that, in business, estimates usually have to be very approximate: we must not be fooled by the accuracy of the arithmetic. In the last resort personal judgement must also be applied. The figures help, but are not decisive.

Adjustments for final accounts

We shall conclude this chapter by considering at greater length certain practical points that have to be dealt with in the actual accounting records (as distinct from working papers). When a profit and loss account and balance sheet are drafted, whether at the end of a financial year or some shorter period, it is necessary, as we have seen, to make adjustments for liabilities for expenses that are accruing but have not yet been recorded because no bill has been received and payment is not yet legally due; and similar adjustments are made where amounts already paid have purchased benefits extending beyond the end of the period of account. In the first instance these adjustments are usually made in the working papers. Eventually, however, their effect has to be incorporated in the main records.

When the full liability is known in the following period, e.g. when the bill is received, it will include the part accrued at the end of the earlier financial period; the liability (and expense) to be recorded at this later date are, therefore, smaller by the amount previously accrued. Thus, suppose that in a given business the electricity expense accrued at 31 December 1982, the balance sheet date, is £30, and that the electricity bill received later, for the three months ended on 31 January 1983, is £50. It follows that the expense to be recorded in the accounts for the March quarter is £20 (plus, of course, any amount accrued from 1 February to 31 March); and this £20, added to the liability of £30 at 31 December, raises the liability at 31 January to the amount of the bill, £50.

Again, at the end of a period one of the assets may be a payment in advance, representing the accrued value of benefits already paid for but not yet enjoyed; when the benefits are enjoyed in the next period this asset must be reduced and a corresponding expense recorded. Suppose that the amount of rent paid in advance at 31 December, representing the benefits of occupation from 1 January to 28 February, is £40. It follows that in the accounts for the March quarter the rent expense must include this £40, and during this period the asset value recorded at 31 December, under the head of payments in advance, will disappear.

If we use special liability and asset accounts in the book-keeping system to record, respectively, the amounts accrued and paid in advance at the balance sheet date, we usually reverse the book-keeping entries immediately after that date in order to eliminate the amounts in question from those accounts in such a way that the amount accrued or paid in advance is left as a credit or debit in the *expense* account in the new period;* this is demonstrated in the following examples, in which the figures are the same as those used above. We shall assume the bill for electricity to 31 January is paid on 14 February. We show only the expense accounts and the asset or liability accounts for payments in advance or accruals.

Accrual:

Electricity expense

1982		£	1982		£
31 Dec	Balance b/d	x	31 Dec	Profit and loss	$(30+x)$
	Electricity Board	30			
1983			1983		
31 Jan	Electricity Board	50	1 Jan	Electricity Board	30

Electricity Board

1983		£	1982		£
1 Jan	Electricity expense	30	31 Dec	Electricity expense	30
			1983		
14 Feb	Cash	50	31 Jan	Electricity expense	50

* The object is to simplify the formal book-keeping or data processing routine, discussed in Chapter 10.

Payment in advance:

Rent expense

1982		£	1982		£
31 Dec	Balance b/d	y	31 Dec	Rent in advance	40
				Profit and loss	$(y-40)$
1983		—			
1 Jan	Rent in advance	40			

Rent in advance

1982		£	1983		£
31 Dec	Rent expense	40	1 Jan	Rent expense	40

It is often considered simpler, however, to make all end-of-period adjustments of the above type in the expense accounts themselves; the ledger accounts for the above examples would then appear as follows:

Electricity expense

1982		£	1982		£
31 Dec	Balance b/d	x	31 Dec	Profit and loss	$(30+x)$
	Balance c/d	30			
1983		—			
31 Jan	Electricity Board	50	31 Dec	Balance b/d	30

Electricity Board

1983		£	1983		£
14 Feb	Cash	50	31 Jan	Electricity Board	50

Payment in advance:

Rent expense

1982		£	1982		£
31 Dec	Balance b/d	y	31 Dec	Profit and loss	$(y-40)$
				Balance c/d	40
31 Dec	Balance b/d	40			

Here the electricity expense account is also acting as a creditor account at balance sheet date, and the rent expense account is also acting as an asset account at that date. (In practice an account for the creditor is sometimes dispensed with at all times, the cash payments being debited directly to the expense accounts.)

The same kind of problem arises in connection with revenue received in advance. If a revenue, such as rent receivable from the letting of property, is received in advance of the services yielded in exchange for it, it is conventional to regard the amount 'unearned' (calculated by making a time apportionment) as measuring the liability to provide those services in the following period: the cash has been received, but there is still a liability to provide services. So a credit balance is carried down, as shown below. This is called *matching expense and revenue*. Assume that a shop owned by the business is let and that on 31 December 1982 rent of £900 is received in respect of the three months to 31 January 1983. If final accounts are prepared at 31 December, a balance of £300 would be carried down at that date, and the revenue to be credited to profit and loss account would be reduced to £600. Such a balance is sometimes called *deferred revenue*.

The account would be:

Rent receivable

1982		£	1982		£
31 Dec	Profit and loss	600	31 Dec	Cash	900
	Balance c/d	300			
			31 Dec	Balance b/d	300

Accruals of revenue can also arise. Their treatment is analogous to that of accruals of expenses.

E

10 Control accounts*

General

Textbooks on book-keeping and accounts have traditionally devoted a good deal of space to what are called the *books of original entry*: the books or other records in which the raw data are assembled and classified before they are entered in the formal double entry system of ledger accounts. On the other hand, our primary interest in this book is in the general principles of double entry book-keeping, and in the balance sheet and profit and loss account, rather than in the original records and sources of information. However, a general appreciation of the process of data collection and classification which links the raw data to the formal accounting system seems likely to be useful, even for those readers who are not concerned with technical accounting details. Those who wish to proceed later to the study of book-keeping and data processing systems in greater detail should understand the nature of the link between the formal accounting system and the sources of accounting data.

We shall indicate here the overall pattern of modern accounting systems. Our discussion will be general and will be appropriate to both electronic data processing systems and traditional handwritten ones. In particular, it will introduce the concept of control accounts, fundamental in any modern accounting system.

Control accounts

The formal double entry system that we have studied in the earlier chapters is the basis of virtually all modern accounting systems. Many of the ledger accounts making up the system must be regarded as what are called *total* or *control* accounts. That is, they summarize a set of transactions that are also recorded in greater detail in what

* This chapter can be omitted by those not interested in the detail of the book-keeping process without impairing their chances of understanding the remaining chapters.

may be called *subordinate* or *detailed* ledger accounts, that is, in ledger accounts that have the same form as the control accounts, but are not part of the formal double entry system.* Let us take a simple example. In a particular business the double entry ledger control account for trade creditors, for one day, appears as follows:

Trade creditors

	£		£
Cash	400	Balance b/d	2,000
Balance c/d	1,900	Stock	300
	2,300		2,300
		Balance b/d	1,900

On examining the detailed subordinate accounts of the trade creditors ledger we find three accounts, each in the name of a separate person, which for the same day appear as follows:

J. Brown

			£
		Balance b/d	1,600
		Stock	200
			1,800

J. Doe

			£
		Stock	100

R. Roe

	£		£
Cash	400	Balance b/d	400

The opening balances of the three subordinate accounts sum as follows:

	£
Brown	1,600
Doe	–
Roe	400
	2,000

* Some accountants may prefer an alternative interpretation, whereby the detailed accounts are part of the formal double entry system and the control accounts are memorandum records. This does not affect the accounting procedures, but is less elegant as a theoretical basis than the interpretation we adopt here.

This total agrees with the opening balance of the control account.

The purchases of stock from these suppliers sum as follows:

	£
Brown	200
Doe	100
Roe	–
	300

This total agrees with the figure shown for stock purchases on the credit side of the control account.

The cash paid to the creditors is as follows:

	£
Brown	–
Doe	–
Roe	400
	400

This total agrees with the control account debit for cash.

Finally the closing balances of the subordinate ledger, when extracted, agree in sign and magnitude with the balance of the control account:

Credit balances

	£
Brown	1,800
Doe	100
Roe	–
	1,900

These three accounts stand for what in practice may be a very large number of individual accounts, all relating to one class of liability, the entries in which are summarized by the entry of totals in the control account.

This relationship between the control accounts (which provide directly the data for reports for management, shareholders, and others) and the detailed subordinate ledger accounts is typical of modern accounting systems.* The detailed accounts provide a legal and arithmetical proof for the total or control accounts, and form the basis for the day-to-day control over such matters as payments to creditors, collection of money from debtors, security of cash and raw materials, and so on. The control accounts accumulate the main accounting magnitudes which have relevance for overall financial control and for certain legal purposes (such as tax assessment). By virtue of the way in which their compilation is organized, the two types of account provide a mutual check on one another's accuracy.†

We can, therefore, when we use balance sheets and profit and loss accounts, reflect that the numerical aggregates that appear under the various headings are supported by a host of detailed records which follow in principle the same general form as those we have described in earlier chapters.

In order to demonstrate more fully the way in which the contents of the ledger control accounts, and of the detailed accounts they summarize, are related, and how both are derived from the records that form the statistical raw material of the accounting process, we shall now consider at greater length the process of building up the creditors control account, the detailed accounts of the creditors ledger (each class of items in which, when summed, gives an item in the control account), the stock control account, and the detailed accounts of the stock ledger.

This description will be as general as possible: it will show the features likely to be common to most good systems whether manual, machine or electronic. It will not describe a particular system. If the principles are understood, students will find they have little difficulty in applying them to other sections of the business, and to particular situations.

The design of the data flow system

Let us suppose that we have to design an appropriate system and are now considering some typical transactions with this in mind. The primary evidence of a purchase will usually be the supplier's invoice (bill) for the goods in question. Our first step must be to arrange a

* It should be emphasized that, though the detailed accounts will have a one-to-one correspondence in pattern with the control account, the actual physical form of both may vary widely, from written traditional ledger pages to impressions on magnetic tape.

† This is part of what is called *internal control*.

procedure whereby invoices, as they are received, are checked for accuracy with respect to the following points:*

1 the actual delivery of the goods, in good condition and in conformity with the specification in the original order to the supplier;
2 the price;
3 the arithmetical accuracy of any calculations and additions.

The invoice must also be checked off against the purchasing department's record of goods ordered, to show that the order has now been satisfied.

The total of the invoice can now be entered in the accounting system. Let us suppose that 100 such invoices, all checked and passed for entry in the books, have been accumulated and that the total value of the invoices has been obtained, e.g. on an adding machine. We have to ask ourselves how much of the information on the invoice needs to be recorded and in what manner. The principles we have studied in the earlier chapters tell us that the effect of the transaction on the balance sheet, and therefore in the double entry system, must be (*a*) to increase stock and (*b*) to increase trade creditors. If an invoice is for £100, the ledger entries, described in T account form, are:

	Stock			*Trade creditors*	
	£	£		£	£
Creditors	100	–	–	Stock	100

or, if described in journal form:

Stock	£100	
Trade creditors		£100

The date of the transaction may be important. We may wish to know whether it falls before, or after, a given date which happens to be the end of an accounting period. We may also wish to maintain a record of the dates of transactions with particular suppliers, e.g. because this affects the date when payment is due. Hence we must record the date assigned to the entry explicitly† or else make sure

---

* In a good system each unit of clerical or accounting work is assigned to a particular person, so that responsibilities are always clear.

† This need not be the actual day the entry is made.

that each transaction can be indirectly identified with a date, e.g. by allotting to each entry a distinctive code number, or by classifying entries in sets all of which can be seen to fall within given time limits. (This could be done by entering all the February items of an account in a section of the account identified with February.)

We shall also want to identify particular entries with (*a*) the supplier's name and (*b*) the type or types of goods. (An invoice for one total amount, identified with one supplier, may relate to several different types of stock.)

We can achieve these aims by:

1 Entering the total value of all our invoices on the credit side of the control account for *trade creditors*, with the date noted.
2 Entering the total value of all our invoices on the debit side of the control account for *stock*, with the date noted.
3 Entering the total value of the invoices relating to a given supplier, say *X*, on the credit side of the subordinate creditors account for *X*, with the date noted, and similarly for all other suppliers in the batch.
4 Entering the total value of the invoices relating to the stock of a given good, say *M*, on the debit side of the subordinate stock account for *M*, with the date noted, and similarly for all other types of stock in the batch.
5 Providing procedural checks as part of the routine of work to ensure that the total value of all items entered under each of 1, 2, 3 and 4 is the same as the original total value of the invoices.

Traditionally, this procedure was carried out by the use of special journals or *day books*, which provided for the analysis and arithmetical check needed; now it is more likely to form part of a system of mechanical or electronic accounting.

The traditional term 'entry' has been used as a shorthand expression for 'making a specified record'. This record need not be written. In the case of 3 above, for example, it may be convenient to use the invoices themselves, suitably sorted and filed, for the record of the amounts owing to each individual supplier. Or the records for 3 and 4 could take the form of punched cards derived from the original invoices, while 1 and 2 were typewritten cards or sheets, obtained by tabulating the punched cards.

The detailed records of 3, combined with all other such records, would constitute the creditors ledger (sometimes called the *purchases* or *bought* ledger). The total in this ledger, for each type of entry in a given period, must sum to the amount of the same type of entry in the creditors control account in the same period.

Similarly the detailed records of 4 support the totals in the stock control account.

These procedures are illustrated in diagrammatic form in Diagram 1. In this diagram the control accounts, forming part of the formal double entry system from which the balance sheet is built up, are enclosed in square boxes. Subordinate ledger accounts are not so enclosed.

The general outlines of data flow systems for other types of transaction are sketched out in Diagrams 2 to 5. These are drawn up on the same lines as Diagram 1 and should be interpreted accordingly. They relate respectively to records of expenses and expense creditors; of sales and debtors; of cash receipts; and of cash payments. These, together with Diagram 1, cover the main aspects of a simple trading company which maintains systematic stock records.*

The extension of these principles to special cases should cause little difficulty once the general pattern is understood.

It may be noted that Diagram 2 differs from Diagram 1 only in that it relates to expenses and expense creditors. No question of

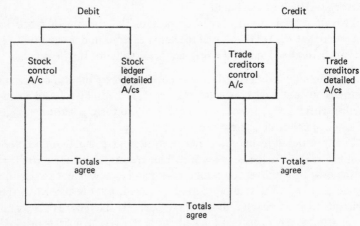

Diagram 1　*Purchases. Source of information: suppliers' invoices*

* It is not always practicable to maintain continuous stock records in detail, though it is best to do so where possible. If such records are not kept, the system for purchases will be similar to that shown in Diagram 2 for expenses, the debits being made, in total only, to an account or accounts for purchases.

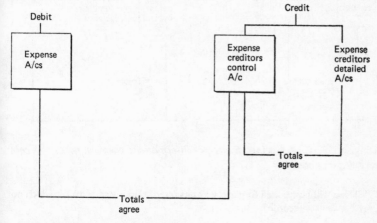

Diagram 2 *Expenses. Source of information: suppliers' invoices*

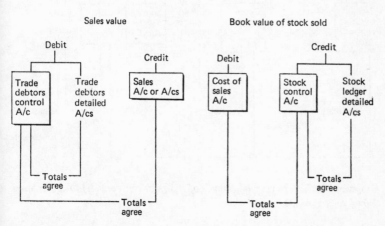

Diagram 3 *Sales. Source of information: copies of sales invoices sent to customers*

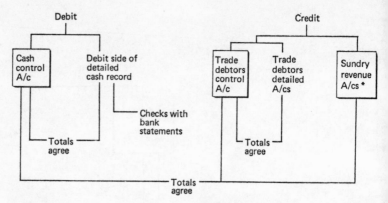

Diagram 4 *Cash receipts. Source of information: cheques, notes and coin received and banked*

* These will be credited for such items as interest on investments for which no previous debt is recorded.

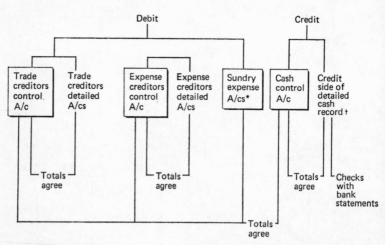

Diagram 5 *Cash payments. Source of information: counterfoils of cheques drawn for payments*

* These will be debited for expenses in respect of which no previous liability has been set up.

† Such payments as wages will be shown in total on the day of payment and will be supported by detailed schedules.

stock arises in this case. The debits are made directly to the main expense accounts. Detailed subordinate accounts are less likely to be needed for the debit aspect of expenses and are not shown in the diagram, though they could be used as a means of reducing the detail in the main ledger accounts. A main double entry ledger account – enclosed in a square in the diagrams – is only described as a 'control account' where there are detailed subordinate accounts supporting it.

Diagram 3 gives the system for sales and debtors. It is in some respects similar to Diagram 1 looked at from the viewpoint of a seller rather than a buyer, but in it the recording, at cost price, of the goods removed from stock is separated from the recording of the sales value. This is necessary in order to obtain separate profit and loss account classifications for sales and for cost of sales.

11 Interpretation

The meaning of interpretation

The purpose of business accounting reports is to provide numerical information that will help the management, the shareholders or other owners, or other interested parties, to make decisions. The analysis and interpretation of these reports is the critical study of the figures they contain carried out with this purpose in mind. As business (or any other set of economic activities) is a process over time, it follows that the study of change and rates of change in figures is in general more informative than the examination of values at a given moment of time: trends are usually more important than absolute figures.

One of the aims of the analysis is to isolate the causes of changes in revenues and expenses and in the balance sheet structure of assets and liabilities; it is therefore essentially a matter of studying relationships. If, for example, sales revenue rises, the board of directors will wish to know how far this is due to a good sales staff. They therefore compare the change in sales revenue with the change, if any, in the expense of the sales organization. A rise in the ratio of revenue to expense is prima facie evidence of higher economic efficiency. The difficulty is that usually other things are changing at the same time. In the above example, changes in general market conditions or in production quality, both of which may affect sales revenue, may confuse the issue. This is why interpretation is difficult and no single test is, in general, significant, taken by itself.

Any accounting figure can be related to another figure or figures, in:

1 a previous forecast or budget;
2 an accounting report for a previous period;
3 the same accounting report;
4 an accounting report of some other organization.

Furthermore, any figure can be considered in connection with events inside or external to the enterprise that are not represented by accounting data. The latter point is especially important because no accounting figures can be interpreted with safety unless the general circumstances of the organization at the relevant times are borne in mind.

The results of analysis can be used in two main ways. They can be used in planning future action; and they can be used to determine whether in the past there has been success or failure to make the best of the economic opportunities, and on whose part. For the first of these uses one may assume that relationships discovered will hold good in the future, subject to adjustments in respect of known changes in conditions: for example, one may decide that a certain relationship between the level of advertising expenditure and sales will persist. In the second use one is in essence considering, on the basis of earlier experience (as where a ratio between two figures changes over time), or on the basis of one's knowledge of the current circumstances, whether relationships discovered indicate a satisfactory state of affairs. One may, for example, after comparing the expenditure on salesmen's salaries and commission for the last three years with the sales revenue for the same period, decide that the results are unsatisfactory, or are becoming less satisfactory. We must never forget, however, the point made above – that there are nearly always many causes operating, and that the apparent cause may not be the true explanation; in the above case the real trouble might be defective products, or a general economic recession.

These two approaches to the study of financial reports correspond to the two main applications of management accounting techniques – estimating and budgeting on the one hand, and cost control on the other. We are thus led to the conclusion that there is no hard and fast distinction between management accounting and financial accounting, though we tend to speak about the former when we are concerned with the analysis of particular activities within the enterprise, and of the latter when we are concerned with the overall results of the enterprise.

It is, however, characteristic of the interpretation of accounts that it is often carried out in circumstances where the results will not lead to action within the enterprise, whereas costing studies are normally intended to result in such action. A minority shareholder in a company can interpret the annual accounts that the directors must send him. But if he dislikes what he finds he can do little except sell his shares. Even this distinction is not always valid. A shareholder who held a controlling interest in his company – a shareholding that carried a substantial part of the voting power in shareholders' meetings – could bring effective action to bear on the directors if his interpretation of the company's accounts led him to believe this was desirable.

The form of reports to be analysed

One of the first steps in analysing profit and loss accounts and balance sheets for a number of periods is to arrange them in columnar form (if they have not been drafted in that form), so that each class of figures that relates to a significant activity of the business can be seen as a series over time. It is not always easy to decide, however, how this is to be done. Alternative classifications are possible; it may be desired, for example, on the one hand to study the total expenditure on advertising particular products in relation to the total sales revenue from those products, and on the other hand to relate the total cost of particular sales departments (each covering a number of products) to their individual sales results. The first type of study requires classification of expenditure by the kind of service purchased – here advertising – and by products; the second by departmental activities inside the enterprise. More than one arrangement of the figures is needed in such a case. Again it is not always easy to decide whether a particular type of transaction should be in a separate class by itself. At what point, for example, are sales revenues from exceptional transactions sufficiently abnormal to be shown separately? No final answer can be given on this. It is a problem in some respects like that of designing experiments in scientific work: in the last analysis it depends upon the nature of the enterprise, its special problems, and the attitudes of those who use the figures.

There is often a temptation to provide a relatively fine or detailed analysis in order to avoid the covering up of relevant information; but it is all too easy to reduce reports to an unmanageable mass of detail: one of the main purposes of accounting is to reduce extensive data to a relatively simple form in order to simplify interpretation. This problem can to some extent be dealt with by preparing reports in such a form that the primary statement – say a profit and loss account – is a relatively simple document without a great number of classifications, and by providing supporting schedules in which the primary figures are analysed in substantially greater detail, and possibly in alternative ways.

It is sometimes useful to select a limited number of key figures which can be presented at frequent intervals to those concerned with management, the object being to convey a good general idea of how things are going without including an excess of detail, the study of which will take up valuable time. Such figures may not by themselves tell anyone much about what is happening in the business unless a good deal is known already; but where this is the case they may be very useful. Thus, a director or a manager might well wish to see the full profit and loss account at least once each quarter; but for the intervening months he might be content to receive a simple statement of the sales revenue and the gross and net profit figures, and the percentages of the latter to the sales revenue. If these seemed satisfactory – that is, if they tallied reasonably well with expectations – there would be no need to spend further time on the figures. If they were not satisfactory, more detailed figures could be called for.

Note that for proper interpretation, the accounting classification of assets and liabilities, and revenues and expenses, should remain on the same basis throughout the period of comparison; accountants must always bear this in mind when they are preparing reports and setting up accounting systems to provide the data for these.

Ratios and approximations

The elementary statistical device of expressing one figure as a ratio of another has the great advantage of simplifying the study of relationships. Suppose that one finds the sales revenue (the 'turnover') of a business has been as follows over the last four years (in £s):

$$11,263 \qquad 15,372 \qquad 18,986 \qquad 23,600$$

The percentage relations, with the first figure expressed as 100, bring out the trends more clearly than the original figures:

$$100 \qquad 136 \qquad 169 \qquad 210$$

One should always be ready to round off figures where this is appropriate; accountants in the past acquired a bad name for their insistence on a higher degree of apparent accuracy than is needed, and often than is significant. In the above comparison the omission of the last three figures makes the interpretation easier without injuring the analysis. We then have:

$$11,000 \qquad 15,000 \qquad 19,000 \qquad 24,000$$

Comparison of actual and budgeted figures

Of the four ways mentioned above in which accounting figures can be related to one another for the purpose of interpretation, the first was the comparison of the figures for a given period with a previous forecast or budget for the same period. This kind of comparison, when carried out systematically, is part of the management technique known as budgetary control. This is an important and interesting subject but to investigate it at length would take us outside the scope of this book. It will, however, be useful to make a few comments on this topic before we leave it.

The comparison of results with a previous budget will usually show that the organization has done better or worse than was anticipated in the budget. This can of course mean that the budget estimates were wrong; or that the organization has been more, or less, efficient than was expected; or that changes have occurred in outside conditions which could not reasonably have been foreseen when the budget was drafted. A variation from the budgeted figure can itself tell us nothing: it can only suggest that further inquiries may be fruitful. Indeed, a close agreement between budget and results may mask unsatisfactory conditions: circumstances may have changed in such a way that results ought to have been better than forecast; or there may have been both bad budgeting and unsatisfactory results, one compensating for the other. The preparation of most budgets requires the cooperation of those who will be responsible later for the actual results and an inefficient subordinate has an interest in setting his target low.

Relationships between reported figures

We turn now to analysis by relating different reported figures of a given business to one another. We shall illustrate this with a simple example, taking the accounting reports of a small company for two successive periods.

The accounts to be analysed are set out in columnar form in

Table 11.1 with an additional column for the changes, absolute and relative, from one year to the next. Other relationships examined are shown in Table 11.2.

Sales revenue and gross profit

We start with the profit and loss account. The first figures relate to sales. The sales revenue has increased over the two years by £1,200, or a little less than 12 per cent. On the face of it this is a good sign, suggesting (unless the whole increase is merely due to a rise in the price level)* that the company is growing, but it is not a conclusive sign that profit is improving, for costs may have risen more. A person not already aware of the kind of change that might have been expected to occur can do little more at this point than mentally note the change, then passing on to the following items. To anyone, however, who has the original plans of the company in mind, or who has some idea of the growth to be expected, the actual increase will have rather more significance, for it should suggest that the company has done as well as, better, or worse than was expected. The next step, therefore, would be to look for reasons. Even so, however, a final opinion must be reserved until the remainder of the figures have been examined.

The next item is the cost of sales, defined as in earlier chapters. This, we notice, has risen by £1,000 or rather more than 12 per cent. There is in consequence a rise in gross profit of £200 (£1,200 *less* £1,000). It is not unreasonable to expect that a rise in sales revenue will bring a corresponding rise in the cost of sales; if more goods have been sold, total costs will usually be higher; if the sales revenue has been raised by a rise in selling prices, it is likely that the prices of the goods bought will also have risen. Whether the rise in cost is a reasonable one having regard to all the circumstances for the two years we cannot tell without further investigation. Again, the existence of earlier estimates may help us. In the final analysis, however, we must go behind the figures and study the circumstances of the changes.

It is useful at this point to examine the relationship between cost of sales and sales; this relationship can be expressed either in the form of the ratio of cost of sales to sales, or of the ratio of gross

* Unless one is using current cost accounts (see Chapter 12), it may be worth while recomputing the sales increase on a constant price level basis by applying an appropriate price index to the figure for one year or the other.

profit to sales. It is often more convenient to use the latter ratio, as businessmen tend to think in terms of this. In our example the ratio of gross profit to sales is 19·6 per cent in 19x1 and 19·3 per cent in 19x2, as Table 11.1 shows. This change might be due to one or more of a number of causes. For example, it could have been caused by a rise in the average cost of goods purchased in relation to the average price of goods sold; it would then be necessary to ask why this had happened: the selling departments might be under-pricing or the buying department might have been less successful than before. Or the fall could be due to the loss or theft of stock so that what appeared to be the cost of sales was in part the cost of stock lost or stolen. Or there might have been a change in the mix of stock sold, in the sense that proportionately more goods carrying lower percentage rates of gross profit had been sold in the second year. These possibilities are not exhaustive. Nor does it follow that a fall in the gross profit percentage is bad in itself. It is the total gross profit that is important.

Table 11.1 *Profit and loss accounts*

	19x1 £	19x1 %	19x2 £	19x2 %	Change £	Change %
Sales	10,200	100·0	11,400	100·0	+ 1,200	+ 11·8
less Cost of sales	8,200	80·4	9,200	80·7	+ 1,000	+ 12·2
Gross profit	2,000	19·6	2,200	19·3	+ 200	+ 10·0
less Administration	730	7·2	790	6·9	+ 60	+ 8·2
Selling and distribution	510	5·0	540	4·7	+ 30	+ 5·9
Finance	310	3·0	400	3·5	+ 90	+ 29·0
	1,550	15·2	1,730	15·2*	+ 180	+ 11·6
Net profit	450	4·4	470	4·1	+ 20	+ 4·4
add Undistributed profit of previous years	900		1,155		+ 255	
	1,350		1,625		+ 275	
less Dividend for year	195		165		− 30	− 15·4
Undistributed profit at end of year	1,155		1,460		+ 305	

* The total does not equal the sum of the individual items because these have been rounded off.

Balance sheets

	31.12.x1		31.12.x2		Change	
	£	£	£	£	£	£
Fixed assets						
Premises, at cost		2,380		2,510		+130
Furniture, fittings and fixtures, at cost	1,780		1,830		+ 50	
Depreciation	310		400		+ 90	
		1,470		1,430		− 40
		3,850		3,940		+ 90
Current assets						
Stock*	1,001		1,580		+579	
Trade debtors	1,460		1,513		+ 53	
Cash	78		67		− 11	
		2,539		3,160		+621
		6,389		7,100		+711
Current liabilities						
Trade creditors		2,234		2,640		+406
Net assets		4,155		4,460		+305
Ownership interest						
Share capital		3,000		3,000		–
Retained profit		1,155		1,460		+305
		4,155		4,460		+305

* Stock at the end of the previous year was £851.

The elasticity of demand may be such that total net revenue is increased by reductions in prices.

This reminds us again that accounting data rarely give us a definite answer to questions, but can suggest lines of investigation. It should be noted, too, that if, for example, a gross profit percentage has not changed it does not necessarily mean that there should be no investigation. Failure to change may mean that something that has been planned has not happened, or that two changes have happened in opposite directions, one tending to raise the percentage and one tending to lower it, so that the final percentage is unchanged. Nevertheless, there is a presumption that further investigation is not necessary if the percentage is unchanged, provided that this is what was expected.

Overhead expenses

In the next section of the profit and loss account are the various overhead expenses relating to different activities of the business. It is characteristic of such expenses that they are unlikely in the short run to change in direct proportion to the change in sales, whereas the cost of sales will often vary in direct proportion with sales, and is in any case likely to be much more sensitive to changes in sales. Even so, it is usually of some interest to relate each head of overhead expense to the level of sales. This is particularly true of the selling and distribution expenses, the size of which may reasonably be expected to be more closely correlated with the level of sales revenue than the other expenses. In our example, it can be seen by inspection that administrative expenses, and expenses of selling and distribution, have risen, though less proportionately than sales. A full interpretation of the increases would require, as usual, a more detailed investigation. However, if the business is growing, as the rise in sales suggests may be the case, it is not unreasonable to expect a gradual increase in such expenses. If, on the other hand, the rise in sales and cost of sales is due to rising prices, it can be expected that administrative expenses and the other expenses will also rise, but possibly at a slower rate, since they will consist of such items as salaries and rents.

Financial expenses have risen much more than in proportion to the other changes. The main items under this head are likely to be interest charges and, possibly, cash discounts to customers. If the business is expanding, we might indeed expect that more finance would be needed and that interest charges might rise. We shall defer further consideration of this item until we have examined some of the balance sheet changes.

The total of the overhead expenses has risen by £180. The net profit therefore has risen by only £20, the increase of £200 in gross profit having been almost absorbed by the rise in those expenses. The percentage of net profit to sales has in consequence fallen from 4·4 to 4·1.

Fixed assets

We now turn to the balance sheets. The first item is that of premises. Here there is an increase, over the two years, of £130. A change of this kind may be important when the future profitability of a business is under consideration. Increases in some or all of the various classes of fixed assets may suggest that future profitability, as new assets come into use, is likely to be greater than that shown in the current profit and loss account. On the other hand, it is also possible for such increases to lag behind the increase in profitability. A business may be able in the short run to increase its activity, and report higher profits, by straining its resources – over-running machinery and so on – in a way not possible in the longer run.

The next item is the furniture, fittings, and fixtures. Here there is a net fall of £40. This is compounded of an increase of £50 in the original cost and an increase of £90 in the depreciation. This tells the reader that there has been expenditure of £50 on the assets in question during the year (after deducting receipts from assets sold, if any). This, too, points to growth in the scale of the business, especially when taken in conjunction with the expenditure on premises, and this may imply growth in the profit in future, as noted above.

The increase in the depreciation figure merely reflects the fact that the assets existing at the beginning of the year are nearer to the end of their useful life; and the figure may include some allowance for fall in value of the new assets bought during the second year.

We know already that the balance sheet value of the fixed assets is not necessarily a good guide to the current realizable value of the assets in the market. The balance sheet does, however, remind us that the assets in question exist and gives some idea of the order of magnitude of their value; this at least gives us the opportunity to make further inquiries. We might think this desirable, for example, if it seemed possible that the company would be liquidated in the near future, if we were considering what security the company could offer for loans, or if we were attempting to estimate the rate of return being earned on the current disposable value of the business's assets.

Current assets

We now come to the current assets. There has been a substantial increase in stock, a small increase in trade debtors, and a small fall in cash. We might well have expected increases in both stock and debtors, since we already know from the profit and loss account that there has been an increase in sales. One expects that to sell more one will have to carry more stock and, if the whole or part of the sales are on credit, that the trade debtors will tend to be higher too. The drop in cash is also not unexpected, since an expansion in business is likely to drain cash off into other types of asset; we have already seen that there has been expenditure on fixed assets in addition to the increase in stock and trade debtors. The fact that the cash balance seems to be rather low need not in itself cause us alarm, for it may be that the balance sheet date is one at which the cash balance is normally low. The drop as compared with last year is perhaps rather more significant. It is true that the change appears small. But it is significant as a percentage; if we were concerned with the same percentage fall in a cash balance of, say, £1,000,000, the drop would be over £140,000. If the fall continues at the same annual rate for two or three years, it may be necessary to raise additional finance. It may not be too early to begin thinking how this will be done.

Turnover ratios

It is useful to consider the growth of stock and trade debtors in relation to the increase in the sales; one way of making the position clearer is to relate these figures each year to the cost of sales, and to the sales, respectively. For example, in Table 11.2 we have calculated what is sometimes called the 'stock turnover rate', that is the ratio of annual cost of sales to stock. In any given business the amount of stock that is held should generally bear a fairly constant relationship to the amount that is sold. There may of course be changes, depending upon the type of goods that are being sold and the way in which the business is developing; but if there are changes it is interesting to know how large they are and why they occur. In this case we notice that the ratio has dropped from 8·2 in the first year to 5·8 in the second. In other words the stock held at the balance sheet date has risen considerably in relation to the sales for the year. A 5·8 rate can be expressed in another way by saying that stock is 'turning over' during the year approximately once every two months on average.* If the ratio had been exactly six, this would have implied that one-sixth of the value, taken at cost, of the year's sales was held in stock at the end of the year. It will be noted that we are

* 12/5·8=2·1.

Table 11.2   *Ratios*

Stock turnover rate* cost of sales/stock	$8,200/1,001 = 8\cdot2$	$9,200/1,580 = 5\cdot8$
Debtor turnover rate* sales/debtors	$10,200/1,450 = 7\cdot0$	$11,400/1,513 = 7\cdot5$
Creditor turnover rate* purchases/creditors	$8,350/2,234 = 3\cdot7$	$9,779/2,640 = 3\cdot7$

Current ratio
  current assets/current
    liabilities
	$2,539/2,234 = 1\cdot14$	$3,160/2,640 = 1\cdot20$

Liquid ratio
  debtors + cash/current
    liabilities
	$1,538/2,234 = 0\cdot69$	$1,580/2,640 = 0\cdot60$

Ratio of ownership interest
  to total claims
  capital + profit/capital
    + profit + liabilities
	$4,155/6,389 = 0\cdot65$	$4,460/7,100 = 0\cdot63$

Ratio of net profit to average
  ownership interest
  net profit/$\frac{1}{2}$ (opening capital
    + opening profit + closing
  capital + closing profit)
	$450/\frac{1}{2}(3,900+4,155)$
	 $= 11\cdot2\%$
		$470/\frac{1}{2}(4,155+4,460)$
		 $= 10\cdot9\%$

* The inverse gives, as a fraction of a year, the average period of investment in stock, of credit given, or of credit received, as the case may be. The ratios are only first approximations because we are comparing the balance sheet data at a given moment of time with the profit and loss data for the whole of the preceding year.

not here comparing the stock at a given moment of time with the rate of sales at that time; we are comparing stock at the end of the year with the cost of sales for the year. Our measure is therefore a fairly crude one; nevertheless it can give us useful information. The fact that the ratio has fallen may suggest, for example, that the business is expected to expand even faster in the following year and that stock has been increased for this reason. Alternatively, however, it may indicate that mistakes have been made in buying and that an unusually large amount of unsaleable stock is now held. In any case the change calls for investigation unless the reader of the accounts already knows why it has happened. If he was expecting this kind of change, this will confirm his expectations. In either case he will have gained something from studying the accounts.

The debtor turnover rate is calculated in the same way, except that here we compare the total debtors at the end of the year with the sales figure. The debtors figure represents the amounts due from customers in respect of the sales price of goods they have bought and it is therefore appropriate to compare it with the selling value of the goods rather than the cost. Here the ratios are 7·0 and 7·5 respectively. The rise may mean that customers are paying more quickly, or that more customers are paying cash and fewer are buying on credit terms. However, it is the sales towards the end of the year that are responsible for the debts still outstanding at the balance sheet date, and the rise could be due to a change in the time pattern of sales during the year. The ratio is an important figure, and a significant change may suggest serious developments. For example, a big fall in this ratio might suggest that debtors were paying very slowly owing to deterioration in the system of collection or deterioration in the general conditions of trade, or that sales were being forced by selling to people whose credit was bad. A rise in the ratio could imply that business was being conducted more efficiently, debts being collected more quickly; but the quicker collection might have a cost: it might mean that additional cash discounts had to be granted to the debtors to encourage prompt payment, thus increasing financial expenses, or that customers were being annoyed by pressure to pay quickly. In some circumstances such a rise could mean the business was in financial difficulties and was having to take every possible step to raise money.

Finance and liquidity

The total of the assets has risen by £711. The remaining sections of the balance sheet will tell us how this increase has been financed. We look first at the current liabilities. These have increased by £406. This, too, might have been expected, for we have been buying more goods, and it is likely therefore that more will be owing to creditors at the end of the year. Again, we can get some idea of what is happening by comparing the ratios of purchases to creditors at the end of each year. (We must use purchases and not cost of sales, for there have been stock changes. We deduce the purchases figures from the cost of sales and the changes in stocks.) This ratio has remained constant at 3·7 (Table 11.2) and suggests therefore that no inquiry is necessary. If, for example, the ratio had fallen, it would have meant that additional finance was being obtained from creditors by deferring payment for a longer period than before. This might be the result of buying different kinds of goods, or buying from different creditors, but it could also indicate that the business was finding it more difficult to raise money and was attempting to obtain more finance from its trade creditors. In this case the cost of postponement might be the sacrifice of cash discounts – possibly equivalent to a relatively high rate of interest – that would otherwise be obtained on payment of the creditors. This too, therefore, is an important ratio to watch.

The importance of liquidity, that is, the relation of the cash resources presently available, or likely to become available in the near future, to the cash that will be needed in the near future to meet liabilities and buy assets, leads to the calculation of two other ratios. The first, sometimes called the current ratio, is the ratio of current assets to current liabilities. It will be seen from Table 11.2 that in our example this ratio has risen slightly, from 1·14 to 1·20. This indicates a slightly less tight liquid position. It should, however, be considered in relation to another ratio, the liquid ratio, the relation of the 'quick' assets (debtors and cash) to current liabilities. Stock may not be quickly realizable without a substantial price sacrifice. Debtors on the other hand can usually be turned into cash fairly quickly. Hence the liquid ratio gives us a better idea than the current ratio of the extent to which we should be squeezed if we had to pay the creditors off quickly. The liquid ratio has dropped from 0·69 to 0·60. This suggests that the company has become slightly less liquid. That the current ratio has risen is due to the fact that there has been a substantial increase in stock. This change may be significant. The examination of the two ratios draws our attention to it.

There are no definite rules that can tell us whether given ratios are correct. It is sometimes said that the current ratio should not be less than 2 and that the liquid ratio should not be less than 1, but it is doubtful whether this statement has much general significance. In some business, for example, it will be perfectly normal to finance much of the stock by obtaining long periods of credit from the suppliers; where this is the case the current and liquid ratios are bound to be lower than where it is not. A business that buys all its stock on credit terms and sells only for cash may, quite reasonably, have a liquid ratio well below 1 and a current ratio not much above 1. On the other hand, it is true that, other things being equal, higher current and liquid ratios indicate greater financial strength – greater ability to meet a crisis. They also indicate, other things being equal again, lower profitability, since more permanent finance is tied up.* Changes in ratios are usually more significant than absolute levels, for they may suggest the kind of developments that are taking place.

As has already been indicated, the lower that it is possible to keep the current and liquid ratios, the more is the business economizing its liquid resources and the lower are its interest charges likely to be. On the other hand, it may be making sacrifices, in that it is offering cash discounts to its debtors to pay quickly, and abstaining from taking discounts from its creditors because it does not pay them quickly. We have already noticed in the profit and loss account that there has been a considerable increase in financial expenses during the year. As cash discounts given to debtors (less those received from creditors) will probably be classified under financial expenses, this increase might be explained by the kind of points we have just been making. Alternatively the increased interest during the year might be due to having to run an overdraft at the bank for some period during the year.

We have seen that £406 of the finance needed to obtain the increase in assets has come from an increase in trade creditors. The remainder comes from the increase of £305 in the shareholders' interest which has arisen because the 19x2 profit has not been fully withdrawn from the business. Thus more than half of the additional finance has come from creditors as distinct from the ownership interest. It is interesting to calculate the ratio of the ownership interest to the total claims. This ratio is given in Table 11.2 as 0·65 in the first year and 0·63 in the second, the decrease being due to the point we have just made. This ratio is an indicator of the extent to which the business is financed by the owners as distinct from outside sources who would be able to press for payment to the point of legal action if the occasion arose. To this extent, therefore, the ratio is an indicator of the degree of risk that the owners might lose control of the business if there were a period of unsuccessful trading, in which liquid resources were depleted, and additional finance could not be obtained.

* This means that more interest must be paid to longer term lenders or that more ownership finance must be provided per £ of profit.

Rate of return on investment

The final ratio in Table 11.2 is that of the net profit to the average ownership interest during the year. This ratio gives some idea of the rate of return that is being earned upon the capital invested in the business. As a rough approximation the ownership interest is taken as the average of the opening and closing figures. This calculation is in principle of considerable economic significance. An owner of resources is interested in comparing the return on his resources in any particular use with the possible return in other uses. The ratio calculated as we have shown it does not, however, give us necessarily a very accurate measure for this purpose, as it is based on balance sheet values of assets; these are not necessarily good measures of the market value of resources – what could be realized by transferring resources to other uses. However, it does give us a rough idea. This can be improved upon, if desired, by estimating more precisely the market values of the assets, though the ratio cannot take into account the intangible elements, such as the quality of management, that cannot be put effectively into the accounts. More important, perhaps, changes in the ratio from year to year give us an idea of the development of the business from the point of view of the profitability of investing further resources. The ratio must be interpreted carefully, for, as we have already explained, there may be a time lag between the addition of fixed assets to the business and an increase in the return from their use. Nevertheless, taken over a period – preferably more than two years – changes in the ratio are of some significance. Furthermore, although the absolute level of the ratio must be interpreted cautiously, if it is *very* low (or *very* high) in relation to what one would expect when resources were used for other purposes, it may well be significant. For example, if the return is very high this may suggest that it would be profitable to invest more resources in the business. It may also suggest that there is danger from competition which will eventually tend to drive down the rate of return. (In an enterprise which wielded a fairly high degree of monopoly power a high return could indicate that this monopoly power was being used, though, for a number of reasons, this would not be conclusive.) If the return is very low, it suggests that it may be better to close down the business. But the ratio must only be used as a first approximation. If it suggests, because it is unduly high or low, that further inquiry is desirable, more careful valuations should be made of the assets, with particular reference to what they would realize if withdrawn from the business, and attention must be paid to lags of the type we have already indicated between investment and increase in profit. More careful investigation may then confirm the original conclusion or, alternatively, may suggest reasons why it should not be accepted.

We relate profit to average capital employed because normally the capital is growing throughout the year as the result of the profit accumulation, and it would be reasonable, therefore, to expect a lower absolute level of profit at the beginning than at the end of the year. This calculation is only a rough approximation, but it must be remembered that it is of the nature of this type of economic measurement that very fine estimates are not possible.

A figure to which some importance may be attached is the annual percentage growth in net profit (shown in Table 11.1 as 4·4 per cent) and in dividends (which in this example was negative, the dividend of 19x2 being lower than that for 19x1). In more sophisticated analyses, taken over a number of years, these might be expressed as compound interest rates of growth in profit and dividend.

This completes our demonstration of the way in which accounting figures can be interpreted with the object of obtaining a clearer picture of the circumstances and changes that lie behind them. Our main object has been to demonstrate principles and methods of approach, rather than to provide an exhaustive discussion of all the different ways in which data of this kind can be analysed. Indeed it would hardly be possible to provide such a discussion, for there are an indefinitely large number of different ways in which this kind of analysis can be carried out. Nevertheless the ratios we have calculated are widely used, and probably provide as good an approach as any to the problem of interpreting any given set of accounts.

The comparison of the accounting figures of different businesses with the object of throwing light on their comparative efficiency can be carried out in a similar way, and raises similar considerations. Special care is needed in drawing conclusions from such comparisons owing to the difficulty of being sure that like is being compared with like; activities similarly described in the accounting reports and manuals of procedure of various organizations often differ in reality.

Changes in price levels

When interpreting accounts one must pay particular attention to the effect of changing price levels over time, and any consequential distortion of relationships between figures. For example, the ratio of end-year stock to cost of sales may be significantly affected if the price at which stock is bought has been rising. Similarly, the calculated rate of return on investment is affected if assets are still valued on the basis of earlier and lower historical costs. The use of current cost accounting can reduce some of these distortions, as can be judged from the discussion of this method in Chapter 12.

12 Accounting and inflation

Inflation shows up some of the limitations of historical cost accounting (HCA). Asset values based on original cost get rapidly out of date. Costs of sales and depreciation based on out-of-date values of stock and fixed assets become increasingly bad indicators of current opportunity costs. Profit calculations based on out-of-date costs become worse and worse indicators of business results.

Proposals for a switch from HCA to the convention of *current cost accounting* (CCA) are a response to this problem. The CCA convention is an alternative approach to asset valuation and to profit calculation. It does not affect all accounting. The recording of cash, debtors and creditors is not changed. Nor is internal control: the maintenance of checks and controls to prevent loss of assets through negligence or fraud. The principles and methods of double entry are unchanged. Cash budgeting and cash flow statements are little affected. (Cash budgeting has always had to take the effects of inflation into account.)

CCA affects:

1 The values shown in accounts for assets such as stocks and fixed assets whose realizable value is not a fixed money amount.
2 Cost of sales: this depends upon the value set on stock. So if this is changed, cost of sales changes too.
3 Depreciation: this is affected by asset values in a similar way to stock.
4 Ownership interest: this automatically reflects changes in the value of assets.
5 Profit: changes in cost of sales and depreciation alter the profit figure.

The accounting entries for CCA

The basic accounting entries for CCA can be indicated simply in journal form. Taking stock first, let us assume that 100 units have been purchased for cash, at a price of £1 per unit. So we have:

Stock	£100	
Cash		£100

The price now rises to £1·20, so the replacement cost is £120. We check that net selling value (realizable value) is equal to or greater than £120. If so, we write an additional amount into the accounts to bring the recorded value to replacement cost, as follows:

Stock	£20	
Revaluation reserve		£20

If 50 units are now sold, the cost of sales will be recorded as:

Cost of sales	£60	
Stock		£60

The effect of the rise in price has been removed from the profit, which in consequence is reported at £10 less than under HCA.

Now consider a fixed asset, say equipment, which the company buys on 1 January, at the beginning of a financial year, for £1,000. Its useful life is estimated at 10 years with no residual value. It is to be depreciated at 10 per cent a year on a straight-line basis. By 31 December of the same year its replacement cost has risen to say £1,600. We check that the estimated present value of its use in the business is equal to or greater than this amount. If so, we revalue the asset to £1,600. We can represent the initial purchase by the entry:

Equipment	£1,000	
Cash		£1,000

The revaluation on 31 December is expressed by the entry:

Equipment	£600	
Revaluation reserve		£600

The 10 per cent depreciation for the year is then shown as:

Depreciation expense	£160	
Depreciation provision		£160

So the profit will be a further £60 smaller than under HCA. (A more subtle approach, discussed in the literature, calculates the depreciation expense on the mid-year replacement value of the asset.)

The general reasoning underlying CCA is that, so far as possible, asset values in the accounts should reflect business and economic reality. Perfect reflection is not possible because reality must be *someone's* assessment. But one can do better, it is argued, than use out-of-date original cost. The asset value to be used is described as the *value to the business*. Another name is *deprival value*, because it is an estimate of the amount that would just compensate the business if the asset were taken away.

As indicated by the example above, value to the business of stocks can be defined as *current replacement cost or net realizable value, whichever is lower*. Value to the business of fixed assets can be defined as *current replacement cost or present value of the asset's best future contribution to the business, whichever is lower*. (Obviously, a fixed asset's best contribution is sometimes what it would fetch now if sold: its net realizable value now.)

These definitions show that the CCA value formula is like HCA except that we substitute current replacement cost for historic cost. Current replacement cost is the cost of a similar asset now. Hence CCA is a form of what is called *current value accounting*.

However, assets would often not be replaced by exactly similar assets. So by current replacement cost we should normally mean the current cost of replacing the *services* of the asset if we were deprived of it. Which is much the same as what we would spend now to procure those services if we did not possess the asset. It is also a better approximation than historic cost to what new competitors would have to spend to obtain similar services.

The estimates we have to make in order to arrive at these current values call for the same kind of thinking as we have to use in deciding how to use assets, and when to replace them or get rid of them. So CCA is closely related to the process of management decisions. Some people hope its use will stimulate better management decisions. Some managements used methods like CCA for their management accounting for a long time before its use was proposed for financial reporting generally.

The profit reported by the CCA method is generally likely to give a better indication than HCA of how much could be withdrawn from the business in dividends or drawings without reducing the probable level of future potential withdrawals below its present level. This is because the CCA cost of sales and depreciation is generally a better indicator of the amount of finance needed to be retained to maintain the same earnings potential.

Monetary items

We say 'generally' above because the full method of CCA is not yet finally worked out. In certain business situations CCA in the basic form outlined above may mislead unless it is extended. There are differing views on this question. The main point is that when price levels are rising the monetary assets of the business, e.g. debtors and cash, will generally need to be expanded in order to support the same level of business as measured by physical standards. This is because the various asset ratios, such as the debtors/stock ratio, tend to be fairly stable over time. In the same way creditors also will tend to rise as physical stocks rise in price. So more finance is needed for the *monetary assets*, but this may be mitigated by the fact that *monetary liabilities* supply more finance. It is argued that these two effects, which are opposite but not necessarily equal, should both be allowed for in the CCA system. More finance to support an existing level of physical business calls, it is argued, for a reduction in reported profit, while the more that the creditors can rise and provide finance without worsening the current asset/current liability ratio, or the gearing ratio, the less is such a reduction needed. Even some of the increased debit for cost of sales or depreciation may not be needed if creditors provide part of the finance to support the rise in values of physical assets.

These arguments are in effect based on a theory by which 'profit' is what could be distributed without reducing the capacity of the business to continue to produce the same flow of goods or services as before, and while keeping the various financial ratios constant.

Maintenance of real value of owner's interest

Another school of thought accepts a theory of profit measurement which attempts to measure how much would be distributed to owners without reducing the ability which the business had at the beginning of the year to generate future flows of *purchasing power* for the owners. For the purpose of this measurement it is assumed, as an approximation, that the current value (the 'value to the business') of the net assets at a given time is a measure of this ability. In a period when there was no general inflation, this theory would demand no further adjustments than those to fixed assets and stocks (which can change individually in price whether there is inflation or not). As, however, in a period of inflation when *average* prices are rising the

F

currency unit itself loses value – i.e. loses some of its command over goods and services in general – an additional, simple, adjustment is called for, it is argued. This amounts to a 'revaluation' of the opening ownership interest by an amount proportionate to the rise in prices in general during the year. The latter is measured by an index number that takes into account the quantities of goods and services that enter into national consumption. In Britain the general index of retail prices is usually accepted as a reasonable measure for this purpose.

If, for example, the amount of the ownership interest (including all retained profit and reserves) at the beginning of the year was £100,000, and the general price level rose by 20 per cent during the year, an adjustment of 20 per cent would be made as follows:

Profit and loss	£20,000	
Capital maintenance reserve		£20,000

This would show that £20,000 of any gross revenue earned was needed, over and above other current expenses, merely to maintain the shareholder's interest, as measured in up-to-date pounds, before it could be said that profit had been earned. No separate adjustment would be made or needed for monetary items.

The need for this debit to profit and loss would, however, be reduced to the extent by which the stock and fixed assets had risen in value. The rise in money values of these physical assets could indeed be greater than the amount needed to maintain the shareholders' interest under this definition. This could happen because the price of the particular assets could rise by a greater percentage than the general price index; or because part of the assets was financed by short- or long-term creditors; or because of a combination of these reasons. The excess would then need to be shown in the accounts as a 'gain' (otherwise they would not balance). Such a gain would not necessarily be treated as 'profit' in the usual sense, however, because of the inevitable uncertainty about whether the asset valuations – especially those of the fixed assets – would, in the longer run, be justified by earnings. In other words, what is sometimes known as the concept of 'prudence' would suggest that such gains be distinguished clearly in some way from 'normal profits', and not brought into the profit and loss account until realized.

A major argument of those who support the application of a 'general purchasing power adjustment' of this kind to the owner's equity is that (subject to the limitations and uncertainties of balance sheet valuation) it would put all businesses on the same footing for the purpose of measuring relative 'better-offness'.

Full stabilization

A further possibility is the *stabilization* of the accounts. This is a more refined variation of the method just discussed. Under stabilization, all the transactions and adjustments during the year are converted into money of the same purchasing power. This is rather as one converts French francs or German marks into British pounds, only here one converts £s of, say, 31 December 1975 into £s of 31 December 1976. (Each of the former is worth about 1·15 of the latter.) The date chosen can be the end of the accounting period, or the beginning, or some earlier date. Comparisons of transactions at different times are thus freed from distortions due to the changing value of the currency in which they are measured. The method is elegant but is apparently too subtle to be understood by many of those who need to use accounts.

Choice of accounting conventions

When considering these differences of view, one should remember that *no* measure of costs or profit is perfect or 'right' in an absolute sense: these measurements relate to human thoughts, impressions and feelings. There is no precise physical reality to fall back on as there is in measuring, say, the height of a mountain or the output of a generator (though even in such cases the conceptual basis of measurement has to be agreed upon and there is always some degree of approximation). So the choice of accounting method is, in the end, a matter of agreement about what is most useful and understandable.

It may be that the actual choice is less important than is sometimes thought. Whatever method of accounting is used, the figures have to be interpreted before judgements can be made. Good interpretation requires a clear understanding of the particular concepts and methods used in the compilation. If this understanding is present, conclusions can be drawn in the knowledge of the scope and limitations of those concepts and methods.

Exercises

Chapter 1: Introduction

1.1 List the main functions of accounting and describe each briefly.

1.2 'When we speak of profit we should be careful to make clear what kind of profit we are talking about.' Explain this statement.

Chapter 2: Balance sheets

2.1 Draw up your personal balance sheet at the beginning of last week. Then list your personal transactions for the week so far as you can remember them, and prepare:
- (a) a cash statement,
- (b) a statement of income, expenditure on consumption and saving,
- (c) a closing balance sheet.

2.2 Explain why an individual's saving in a period is not necessarily measured by the change in his cash holding in the same period. (Note that 'cash' includes coin, notes and money at the bank.)

2.3 The Inspector of Taxes dealing with A's affairs suspects that A has not declared his full income for the tax year 19x8–9. He therefore asks A to supply a list of his assets and liabilities at 5 April 19x9. He already possesses such a list as at 5 April 19x8. These lists are shown in the table below.

The Inspector also asks A how much he has spent on personal consumption during the tax year. He is told that the amount is £6,000.

You, as the Inspector's assistant, are required to:
- (a) Draw up A's personal balance sheets at the two dates, using the values given.
- (b) Draw up a funds statement for the tax year so far as the information permits and deduce A's income for the year from it as the missing figure in the statement.

(c) Show how much the income deduced in (b) is over- or under-stated if:

   (i) An asset consisting of £1,500 in a savings bank at 5 April 19x8 and spent during the tax year (as part of the £6,000 personal consumption mentioned above) was not known to the Inspector.

   (ii) *A* under-stated his expenditure on personal consumption by £3,000.

(d) State briefly why the values of the assets in the lists are (with the agreement of the Inspector) determined by their cost and not by current market values.

	5 April 19x8	5 April 19x9
	£	£
Assets		
House (cost)	35,000	35,000
Investments (cost)	10,000	13,500
Bank balance	2,500	—
Furniture, pictures, etc. (cost)	12,000	12,000
Car (cost)	4,500	4,500
Second car (cost)	—	4,000
Liabilities		
Building society	15,000	11,500
Bank overdraft	—	500

Chapter 3: Business accounts 1

3.1 Construct an imaginary balance sheet for three of the organizations listed below, showing the classes of assets and liabilities, and the ownership claims, that you would expect to find, and inserting arbitrary values for each class:

   a bus company
   a retail grocer
   a municipal swimming bath
   a society for the abolition of taxation
   a university college
   an aircraft manufacturer
   a film production company
   an atomic energy authority
   a bank

3.2 From the data given below, which refer to a wholesale business, prepare:

(*a*) an opening balance sheet at 1 January,

(*b*) a funds statement for the month, explaining the net change in the cash,

(*c*) a profit and loss statement for the month,

(*d*) a balance sheet at 31 January.

Assets and liabilities at the opening of business on 1 January

	£
Cash at bank	1,420
Trade debtors	410
Trade creditors	260
Stock	3,210

Transactions

			£
January	1	Stock purchased on credit	420
,,	5	Trade creditors paid by cheque	205
,,	10	Stock costing £560 sold on credit for	720
,,	17	Drawings by owner	100
,,	26	Rent of premises paid for month	40
,,	31	Wages paid for month	60

3.3 What is meant by the 'liquidity' of a business?

3.4 What is the difference between 'drawings' and 'expenses', and why are they treated differently in showing the results of a business?

3.5 *A*, a doctor, has the following assets and liabilities relating to his medical practice on 1 January and 31 December 19—:

	1 Jan	31 Dec
	£	£
Surgery equipment	2,765	2,936
Motor car	880	660
Stock of drugs	432	382
Due from Ministry	736	867
Due to creditors	95	69
Cash at bank	79	93

During the year his weekly drawings amounted in total to £1,632, but he paid into the practice bank account a £100 prize received from his private holding of premium bonds.

Prepare opening and closing balance sheets (i.e. at 1 Jan and 31 Dec) and compute the profit (or loss) of the practice for the year on the assumption that all the valuations may be accepted.

Chapter 4: Double entry book-keeping

4.1   What are the fundamental rules of double entry?

4.2   Show the opening entries and transactions of Exercise 3.2 in:
   (*a*) journal form,
   (*b*) T account form.

4.3   A friend says to you: 'Book-keeping is very odd. If you receive some money you debit an account which seems to suggest something bad. If you make a profit you increase the part of the balance sheet where the liabilities are.'

Explain to your friend the logic of the relevant book-keeping entries.

Chapter 5: Form of financial reports

5.1   Summarize the main points of difference between (*a*) sole traders, (*b*) partnerships and (*c*) limited companies, so far as their legal and accounting characteristics are concerned. Set out your summary as a table with three columns.

5.2   The figures given below comprise the double entry ledger accounts of a trading business for the first month of trading, before the insertion of the closing balances at the end of the month. You are required to insert the closing balances in the ledger accounts and prepare two sets of accounting reports for the owner. Each set should be in the form of a profit and loss account for the month, an appropriation account (where relevant) and a balance sheet at the end of the month. Prepare the first set on the assumption that the business belongs to a sole trader and the second set on the assumption that it is carried on as a limited company.

	Stock		Trade debtors		Cash at bank		Capital		Profit and loss	
	Dr	Cr	Dr	Cr	Dr	Cr	Dr	Cr	Dr	Cr
	£	£	£	£	£	£	£	£	£	£
Cash paid in by owner					500			500		
Stock bought	300					300				
Stock sold on credit		200	300							100
Stock sold for cash		50			75					25
Wages paid						40			40	
Rent paid						45			45	
Withdrawn by owner						30	30			

5.3 Repeat Exercise 5.2 for a partnership with two partners, *A* and *B*, where:

(*a*) the opening capital is provided as follows:

    A   £300

    B   £200

(*b*) profits and losses are to be shared as follows:

    A   three-fifths

    B   two-fifths

(*c*) the drawings were divided as follows:

    A   £15

    B   £15

Capital accounts are to be kept separate from current accounts. The appropriation account should be shown.

5.4 List five bodies or authorities whose rules or requirements have to be taken into consideration in preparing company accounts in Britain.

Chapter 6: Business accounts 2

6.1 The data given below relate to a small manufacturing company. From these prepare double entry records for the month, and appropriate accounting reports:

Assets and liabilities, 1 March 19—

	£
Stocks (valued at cost):	
Raw materials	560
Work in progress	227
Finished goods	281
Trade debtors	322
Trade creditors	169
Cash at bank	329
Equipment (valued at cost *less* an estimate	
of loss in value due to wear and tear)	620
Share capital	2,000
Profit and loss account (credit)	170

Transactions

			£
March	3	Sold goods costing £53 on credit	78
,,	6	Bought raw materials on credit	113
,,	7	Paid wages	22
,,	11	Received payment from debtors	162
,,	14	Paid wages	22
,,	16	Completed work on certain products, cost for balance sheet valuation being assessed at	93
,,	21	Paid wages	22
,,	23	Paid creditors	87
,,	24	Sold on credit stock costing £120 for	190
,,	28	Paid wages	22
,,	31	Paid monthly rent	30
		Paid dividend to shareholders	40

During the month raw materials costing £40 were taken out of store for manufacturing purposes.

Half the wages and half the rent are assumed to add to the value of work in progress. The remainder is written off as an administrative expense to profit and loss account.

The loss in value of the equipment during the month is assessed at £5. An equivalent amount of value is assumed to be added to the work in progress.

6.2   Using the same opening data (i.e. at 1 January) as in question 3.5, but ignoring all other data in that question, prepare on the basis of the summarized information given below: (*a*) a set of double entry records for the year; (*b*) a profit and loss report for the year; and (*c*) a closing balance sheet at 31 December.

	£
Debt due from Ministry on 1 Jan received and paid into bank	736
Fees received from Ministry during year (in addition to the above item) and paid into the bank	1,475
Drugs bought from suppliers during year and paid for by cheque	324
Creditors at 1 Jan paid by cheque	95
Value of drugs (valued at cost) used in practice during year	443
Drugs bought from suppliers during year not paid for at 31 Dec	69
Fees due from Ministry not paid at 31 Dec	867
Loss in value of motor car during year	220
Surgery equipment purchased and paid for by cheque during year	171
Drawings during year	1,607

6.3 What is the difference between work in progress valuation at (*a*) direct manufacturing cost of production and (*b*) full manufacturing cost of production? What is the effect on reported profit of using (*a*) instead of (*b*)?

Chapter 7: Current assets and liabilities

7.1 What is a current asset? List the main types of current asset.

7.2 What is the normal historical cost convention for the valuation of stocks?

7.3 What is a current liability?

7.4 What is the difference between a liability and a provision for a liability?

Chapter 8: Fixed assets and depreciation

8.1 *A* starts a business with a capital of £1,150. The business consists of buying automatic vending machines and selling confectionery through the machines.

A withdraws each year the whole of the profit shown by his accounts, but no more. His stock remains constant at £100 (at cost). He always pays cash for purchases. At the end of 5 years *A*'s balance sheet is as follows:

A

Balance sheet, 31 December

	£		£	£
Capital	1,150	Automatic machines:		
		Cost	1,000	
		Depreciation	500	
			——	500
		Stock in machines		
		and in store	100	
		Cash at bank	550	
			——	650
	1,150			1,150

A tells you he cannot understand why his cash balance is so high when he has withdrawn all his profit each year.

Explain to him why this is.

8.2   At what period or periods during a business's life would you expect the needs for finance to be especially high? Explain your answer and if possible illustrate it with simple balance sheets.

8.3   *C* is a dentist. His summarized practice balance sheets at the end of two successive years are:

	Year 1	Year 2		Year 1	Year 2
	£	£		£	£
Capital	1,560	2,050	Equipment (at cost)	1,320	1,700
Creditors	70	120	Fees owing	160	390
			Cash at bank	150	80
	1,630	2,170		1,630	2,170

'Capital' in this case includes original capital paid in and profits not withdrawn.

In Year 2 the profit was £1,390 of which £900 was withdrawn during the year for personal needs.

C complains that there is now not enough money at the bank to allow him to enjoy the balance of his profit.

Write a short letter to him explaining the financial position of the practice.

8.4   What is a fixed asset?

8.5   Should an amount equal to annual depreciation be held in cash? Give reasons.

8.6   What is goodwill? How does it differ from other intangible assets?

8.7   How can goodwill be measured?

8.8   What are trade investments? What different kinds are there?

8.9   What is capital expenditure?

Chapter 9: Problems in double entry and final accounts

9.1   A firm's trial balance on 1 January is as follows:

	£	£
Capital		1,000
Stock	500	
Debtors	300	
Creditors		200
Cash at bank	150	
Equipment (cost)	460	
Depreciation provision		210
	1,410	1,410

During January and February sales are expected to be at the rate of £200 per month and thereafter at £300 per month. Purchases will be at the rate of £160 per month throughout the months January to April.

Debtors balances are due during the second calendar month and creditors balances during the third calendar month after the end of the calendar month in which the sales or purchases, as the case may be, occur. All sales and purchases are for credit.

General expenses of all kinds will require a monthly cash outlay of £30.

In March new equipment is to be bought for £350, payable at once in cash.

The owner will withdraw £20 per month for personal use.

Calculate the cash balance at the end of April assuming that all receipts and payments occur on their expected due date, and prove your answer by preparing a balance sheet at 30 April.

9.2 *A* is starting up a new business on 1 January 19—. He asks you to calculate for him his estimated profit during the first half-year. He provides the following information:

	£
Annual rent of premises, payable quarterly in arrears, first payment due on 31 March	3,600
Cash outlay on equipment – payable 15 January	3,700
payable 15 March	5,400
Monthly planned purchases of stock for re-sale (estimated cost):	
January	15,000
February	25,000
March to June inclusive (per month)	10,000

All stock is bought on two months' credit.

Monthly planned sales (at estimated selling prices):

January	6,000
February	8,000
March	11,000
April–June inclusive (per month)	12,000

Planned selling price each month is on average 20 per cent above cost.

All sales are on one month's credit. No bad debts or arrears of payments are expected.

Monthly cash outlay on general expenses including salaries is expected to be   480

Depreciation of equipment in the first half-year is estimated at 5 per cent of initial cost.

A will pay £30,000 cash into the business. He does not plan to withdraw any money from the business during the year.

Required: (*a*) Budgeted trading and profit and loss account for the half-year, and closing balance sheet, in a form suitable for presentation to management.

(*b*) A statement showing the maximum finance (other than that provided by trade creditors) that will be needed during the half-year, and the amount by which *A*'s paid-in capital exceeds this figure. State the date on which the maximum amount given will be needed. (Assume that all receipts and payments in any given month will occur on the last day of the month in which they fall due.)

Hint: As the question asks for the maximum figure of cash needed (which requires ascertainment of the date of the minimum debit balance) it will be necessary to compute the balance of the bank account at the end of each month.

9.3 At the beginning of 19— a small shipping firm, owned by an individual owner–manager, has the following assets and liabilities:

	£
Motor vessel (at cost)	200,000
Stock of sea-going stores	16,000
Cash at bank	15,000
Debtors (for freight)	14,000
Creditors (for harbour dues and other expenses of voyages)	19,000

During 19— the following transactions (which have been summarized) occur:

	£
Cheques and cash received for freight including £14,000 from the debtors at 1 January 19—	86,000
Payments from bank for expenses of voyages including £19,000 to the creditors at 1 January 19—	28,000
Payments from bank for office and general expenses	11,000
Payments from bank for purchase of stores	26,000
Cash drawn from bank by owner for personal use	2,000
Harbour dues and other voyage expenses incurred in 19—, but not paid at 31 December 19—	14,000

At 31 December 19— the stock of stores held was valued (on cost basis) at £13,800. The difference between this figure and stock previously held and bought during the year is an addition to the cost of voyages during the year.

The depreciation of the ship is estimated on the basis of a straight-line fall in value, over a period of twenty years, to a zero residual value. At 1 January 19— the ship was two years old.

The ship had just begun a voyage at 31 December 19—. Expenses of that voyage (included in the expenses shown above) amounting to £3,500 are to be treated as an asset (like 'work in progress' in a manufacturing business) at balance sheet date. No revenue from this voyage has yet been received or included in the above figures.

Required: Balance sheet at 31 December 19— and profit and loss account for the year. Show all working calculations.

Hint: Start by calculating the opening capital. Then use T accounts and prepare a trial balance as at 31 December 19—.

9.4 Prepare a profit and loss statement for 1980, and a closing balance sheet, from the following data relating to the business of *R*, a sole trader whose accounting records are incomplete:

Summary of bank account for 1980

	£		£
Debtors for goods	4,410	Balance, 1 January	660
Sale of business investment	1,820	Creditors for goods	2,900
		General expenses	980
		Drawings	760
		Balance, 31 December	930
	6,230		6,230

The ledgers that were kept show the following balances:

	£
Close of business 31 December 1979:	
Debtors for goods sold	5,820
Creditors for goods bought	1,640
Furniture, fixtures and fittings	1,890
Investment	1,800
Petty cash	40
Close of business 31 December 1980:	
Debtors for goods sold	6,590
Creditors for goods bought	2,100
Furniture, fixtures and fittings	1,890
Petty cash	60

The depreciation rate for the furniture, fixtures and fittings is 10 per cent on the opening balance each year. Stock in trade at 31 December 1979 was £2,010 and at 31 December 1980, £2,830.

9.5   The following accounting information for 19— relates to the Brightmouth-on-Sea Municipal Opera House:

Ledger balances at 31 December

	£
Surplus on income and expenditure account (as at previous 1 January)	1,252
Musical, stage and other equipment (as at previous 1 January)	1,919
Stocks of food and drink for the restaurant as at 1 January	590
Bank overdraft	530
Liability in respect of money paid for advance bookings	187
Sundry creditors	762
House receipts from sale of tickets (other than advance bookings)	6,732
Catering sales	3,416
Catering purchases	2,437
Salaries and wages (of which £500 refer to the restaurant)	4,938
General expenses, including rent, insurance, interest, etc.	1,762
Expenditure on productions during year	1,233

Additional information:

Stocks of food and drink as at 31 December	229

10 per cent is written off the musical and other equipment annually.

Required: Annual accounts (income and expenditure account and balance sheet) for 19—.

9.6   A business has the following summarized balance sheet at the beginning of 19—:

	£	£
Equipment – cost		1,600
depreciation		600
		1,000
Stock	500	
Debtors	300	
Cash	200	
	1,000	
Creditors	400	
		600
Capital		1,600

The following forecasts are made for this business for the year:

	£
Cash expenditure on replacement of equipment worn out (fully depreciated in the accounts at the beginning of year, i.e. reduced to zero value)	1,100
Sales (including sales of £550 not paid for at end of the year)	4,800
Purchases (including purchases of £650 not paid for at end of year)	3,200
Stock (at cost) at end of year	600
General expenses (all paid in cash)	890
Depreciation	310
Owner's drawings during year	420

Required: Advise the owner:

(a) On the expected financial (i.e. cash) position during the year.

(b) What special action, if any, this position calls for.

9.7 *A* Ltd is a small furniture-making company. Its ledger balances at 1 January 19— are as follows:

	£
Machinery and tools (original cost)	6,000
Provision for depreciation	3,000
Stock of wood (cost)	4,000
Work in progress	6,000
Finished furniture	5,000
Trade debtors	2,000
Cash at bank	1,000
Trade creditors	1,000
Share capital (15,000 shares)	15,000
Profit and loss account	5,000

The transactions for the year following, summarized, are:

	£
Sales to customers on credit	20,000
Purchases of wood from suppliers on credit	4,000
Cash received from customers	21,000
Cash paid to suppliers	3,000
Cost of wood drawn from stock for manufacture	5,000
Cost of furniture finished (calculated as noted below)	13,000
Cost of furniture sold (calculated as noted below)	15,000
Cash paid for production wages	9,000
Cash paid for general manufacturing expenses	1,000
Cash paid for general administrative expenses	2,000
Amount owing to landlord for rent of workshop up to end of year, unpaid at 31 December	1,000
Cash dividend paid to shareholders	1,000

Note: The company values its work in progress and finished goods stock, and calculates its cost of sales, at the direct cost of production (cost of wood and labour only). All other expenditure is treated as current expense for the period to which it relates. Depreciation of machinery, etc., is assessed at 10 per cent per annum on cost.

Required: (*a*) Set of double entry accounts in T form and closing trial balance.

(*b*) Final accounts for the year for report to the shareholders (balance sheet, profit and loss account and funds statement).

9.8   *B* Ltd is an industrial company producing a single product. The company commenced business at the beginning of 19—.

Data for that year are as follows:

Raw material stocks bought: £30,000.
Raw material stocks at end of year at cost:

	£
Material *X*	800
,, *Y*	700
,, *Z*	1,500
	3,000

Material *X* is no longer needed but it could be sold for £700.
Costs for the year (other than raw material):

	£
Wages of direct labour force	28,000
Other manufacturing costs (excluding depreciation)	32,000
Administrative costs	10,000
Selling costs	10,000

Machines used for manufacturing were all bought at the beginning of the year. The cost was £100,000. The estimated useful life is ten years. They will then be sold. The estimated net realizable value then is £20,000.

Total production of finished goods in the year was 100,000 units, of which 10,000 remained in stock at the year end. There was no work in progress at the year end. The selling price per unit during the year was £1·50. However, the products in stock at the year end are only expected to sell for £0·90.

Required: Profit for the year on two alternative assumptions:

(a) if cost of sales and stock value is calculated on the basis of direct production cost;

(b) if cost of sales and stock value is calculated on the basis of full production cost.

Chapter 10: Control accounts

10.1 A firm keeps a detailed creditors ledger, controlled by a creditors control account, and a detailed stock ledger controlled by a stock control account. The stock ledger is kept in quantity as well as value. Issues from stock are valued at cost, making the assumption that the first stock in is the first to leave (the 'FIFO' system).

On 1 March the list of the detailed creditors ledger balances is as follows:

Suppliers	£
A	360
B	20

The detailed stock ledger balances are:

Goods	Items	£
X	18	180
Y	1	20

During March:

(a) B supplies 10 items of type X at £12 each, and 1 item of type Y at £20.

(b) A's account is settled in full.

(c) A later supplies 4 items of type X at £12 each, and 1 item of type Z at £18.

(d) C supplies goods of type Y, 6 items at £22 each.

(e) 9 items of type X are issued from store for dispatch to a customer.

Required: Show the creditors control account and the stock control account for March, and prove the correctness of each by extracting lists of the detailed creditors ledger and detailed stock ledger (value) balances. Draw a diagram showing the flow of information to the clerks or machine operators responsible for the various jobs.

10.2 You, as accountant of a wholesale grocer, are asked by your chief:

(*a*) What did we pay in rent last year?

(*b*) How long have we been dealing with our customer John Brown? Does he pay regularly?

(*c*) How much cash have we at the bank, how much do we owe to creditors and how much do debtors owe us?

(*d*) How many kilos of cayenne pepper have we in stock?

Where would you find the answers to each of these questions:

1 if the accounts were fully up to date;
2 if the accounting work was a month in arrear?

10.3 The double entry accounting system of a business includes a creditors control account which controls a subordinate creditors ledger.

At 31 December the general ledger trial balance debit and credit totals (based on control account balances) are:

Dr	Cr
£	£
6,126	6,245

The credit side of the trial balance includes £862 as the balance of the creditors control account. The list of the subordinate creditors ledger balances adds up, however, to £887.

The following errors are found:

(*a*) The balance of W. Smith, a creditor, has been brought down as £8 instead of £18 in the detailed creditors ledger.

(*b*) £162 that has been debited to equipment account represents a payment for rent.

(*c*) When a batch of suppliers' invoices was totalled in order to provide the figure for the creditors control account, the amounts of two invoices, together totalling £35, were omitted; the creditors ledger machine operator posted the invoices accurately to the subordinate ledger, but failed to check the total of the detail postings against the above control total and the supervisor failed to notice this. The stock ledger and the stock control account were posted correctly, but in neither case was the total checked against the original, incorrect batch total.

(*d*) Invoices for goods supplied, costing £167, have not been received. No record of the purchase or of the receipt of the goods has reached the accounting system, but the goods are in the store.

(*e*) In the account for rent, £77 for rent paid has accidentally been entered on the credit side of the account.

There are no other errors. You may assume that the closing stock value is obtained from the balance of the stock control account after crediting the cost of sales, the latter being independently determined.

Required:

1 What is the correct trial balance total?
2 What is the correct amount of the balance of the creditors control account and of the list of the detailed creditors ledger balances?
3 If the net profit before correcting errors was £500, what is it after the corrections have been made?

In your answer show separately the effect of (*a*), (*b*), (*c*), (*d*) and (*e*) under each head 1, 2 and 3.

10.4 In a given business the sales accounting is organized so that the debtors transactions are recorded in detail in a subordinate sales ledger controlled by a debtors control account in the general ledger. The general ledger includes the whole of the formal double entry system.

A trial balance is extracted from the general ledger and is found not to balance. After investigation the following errors are found:

(*a*) A copy sales invoice for £30 had been mislaid before it reached the accounting department. (The copy invoices provide the sales posting information.)

(*b*) The machinist posted a cash receipt of £67 to the detailed sales ledger as £76 and failed to notice that the total amount of cash receipts posted by her to the detailed ledger did not agree with the initial (correct) control total of the cash receipts summary (which would agree with the control account posting).

(*c*) The discount on sales transactions listed with the cash receipts data was £80. A fly's leg stuck to the paper after the sales ledger machinist had made, and agreed, her detail postings, and the general ledger clerk, when making his general ledger control account postings, read the figure as £180.

(*d*) The debit side of the debtors control account in the general ledger was cast ('added up') incorrectly, the total appearing £10 greater than it should.

Required: Show the corrections to be made respectively to:

1 The debtors control account.
2 The general ledger trial balance.
3 The list of balances of the subordinate sales ledger.
4 The profit and loss account (assuming that revenue and expense balances have already been transferred to it).

10.5   Explain clearly and carefully, making use of diagrams if you think they will be helpful, an accounting procedure for the collection, recording, and classification (i.e. the data processing) of information relating to the following business activities. Show the procedure from the point where the original data becomes available to the completion of the formal double entry records.

1 Sale of goods on credit.
2 Purchase of goods on credit.
3 Receipt and payment of cash (all receipts being banked and all payments being made by cheque).
4 Receipt, store, and issue of goods for sale.

Chapter 11: Interpretation

11.1   Give an interpretation of the following figures, summarized from the accounting reports for two successive years of a company carrying on a wholesale business:

	£000	
	Year 1	*Year 2*
Sales	1,950	2,290
Cost of sales	1,370	1,640
Office and general expenses	246	282
Travellers' commission and expenses	21	26
Running and maintenance costs, and depreciation, of delivery trucks	13	16
Interest on bank overdraft	20	26
	1,670	1,990
Net profit	280	300
Taxation	120	130
	160	170
Undistributed profit from previous year	260	380
	420	550
Dividends on shares	40	80
Profit retained in business	380	470
Property, plant, and equipment:		
Balance from previous year	920	1,070
Additions *less* sales	150	280
	1,070	1,350
Depreciation	400	490
	670	860
Stocks	630	830
Trade debtors	570	690
Cash at bank and in hand	280	380
	2,150	2,760
Share capital, £1 shares	680	1,000
Profit	380	470
	1,060	1,470
Bank overdraft	390	480
Trade creditors	700	810
	2,150	2,760

11.2 A public company selling household equipment has just published its annual accounts for 19x7. The accounts are summarized below with the figures for the preceeding year. Given an interpretation of the accounts for someone who is considering investing in the company's shares.

	£000	
Profit and loss account	*19x6*	*19x7*
Sales	3,929	4,703
Trading profit	1,100	1,505
Depreciation	124	156
Loan interest	—	9
Directors' remuneration	81	83
Auditors' remuneration	5	5
	210	253
Profit before tax	890	1,252
Taxation	463	651
Earned for dividend	427	601
Dividends for year	326	543
Retained for year	101	58

Balance sheet

	19x6	19x7
Share capital – shares of £1 fully paid	1,086	1,086
Retained profit	487	545
	1,573	1,631
Fixed assets		
Land and buildings at cost	339	339
Depreciation	25	28
	314	311
Plant, machinery, equipment and vehicles at cost	1,064	1,261
Depreciation	236	389
	828	872
Total fixed assets	1,142	1,183
Current assets		
Stock, including work in progress, at cost	956	1,407
Debtors	896	1,992
Cash at bank and in hand	432	183
	2,284	3,582
Current liabilities		
Creditors	1,097	2,157
Taxation	463	651
Dividends due to shareholders	293	326
	1,853	3,134
Net current assets	431	448
Total assets	1,573	1,631

Short reading list

There is a vast array of books on accounting and on allied subjects. This list is an attempt to help the learner by indicating a small number of books and journals which can be used to supplement and extend his knowledge. The reading itself, and the references in it, will suggest further sources. The selection of works for inclusion in such a short list must be arbitrary and some good books must be excluded. The non-inclusion of a book does not indicate disapproval.

Financial accounting

H. Bierman and A. R. Drebin, *Financial Accounting: an Introduction* (New York and London, 1972), is perhaps as good a text as any for supplementing and extending an introductory knowledge of the subject. It introduces the basic ideas, with particular reference to business corporations (limited companies), in substantially greater detail than has been possible in this book. It includes a section on compound interest and discounting. As an American text it introduces the reader to terminology and ideas that are important in these days of international companies.

G. A. Lee, *Modern Financial Accounting* (London, 1975), is a comprehensive British text. Its treatment is compressed and one may disagree here and there with its exposition, but I suspect that most university and polytechnic students of the subject (and many others) will have frequent recourse to it.

Accounting theory

By far the best treatise on the fundamentals of financial accounting (including those relating to problems of inflation) is W. T. Baxter, *Accounting Values and Inflation* (London, 1975). No one who really wants to understand the subject can afford to neglect this work. Another useful reference is W. T. Baxter and S. Davidson, *Studies in Accounting* (London, 1977).

E. S. Hendriksen, *Accounting Theory* (Homewood, 1977), provides a comprehensive survey of thought on a wide range of accounting matters from an American viewpoint. This, too, provides many references for further study.

Finance and financial decisions

An extremely good elementary but by no means superficial introduction to business finance, with particular reference to the British scene, is F. W. Paish, *Business Finance* (London, 1978). It is strongly recommended for beginners as a complement to this book.

A first-class introduction to the theory of investment decisions and its relation to accounting will be found in B. V. Carsberg, *Analysis for Investment Decisions* (London, 1974). Another useful book is M. Bromwich, *The Economics of Capital Budgeting* (Harmondsworth, 1976).

Accounting standards

For a reflective discussion of the aims and limitations of accounting standards, see P. A. Bird, *Accountability: Standards in Financial Reporting* (London, 1973).

For details of standard practice in Britain and Ireland, see Institute of Chartered Accountants in England and Wales, *Accounting Standards* (London, 1977). This covers Statements of Standard Accounting Practice, Nos. 1 to 11. Later statements will be available from the same source, and from the other main accounting bodies, as they are issued.

Inflation accounting

Much of the reading on accounting theory is concerned with this subject. Specific reading relating to the British scene will be found in the United Kingdom government publication, *Report of the Inflation Accounting Committee (Sandilands Committee)*, Cmnd. 6225 (London, 1975), and in Inflation Accounting Steering Group, *Guidance Manual on Current Cost Accounting* (London, 1976).

The accounting journals (see below) are a prolific source on this subject.

Accounting and computers

T. W. McRae, *Computers and Accounting* (London, 1976), provides a useful conspectus.

Management accounting

H. C. Edey, *Business Budgets and Accounts* (London, 1966), can be used as an introductory text. For more advanced study, two American texts, C. T. Horngren, *Introduction to Management Accounting* (Englewood, Cliffs, N.J., 1978) and *Cost Accounting* (Englewood Cliffs, N.J., 1977) are probably as good as any.

History of accounting

A. C. Littleton and B. S. Yamey, *Studies in the History of Accounting* (London, 1956), is recommended.

Law

Readers who would like to know something of the background of company accounting will find a useful introduction to company law in J. F. Northey and L. H. Leigh, *Introduction to Company Law* (London, 1971). For an interesting insight into how the modern limited company developed, see the opening chapters of L. C. B. Gower, *Modern Company Law* (London, 1969).

Journals

Almost every country and every professional body has its own journals or journal. The more widely read British journals include:

Accountancy
The Accountant
Accounting and Business Research
Journal of Business Finance and Accounting

American journals concerned particularly with recent thought and study are:

Accounting Review
Journal of Accounting Research

Journal UEC (The European Journal of Accountancy), published in English, French and German, covers European developments and current discussion.

Index